UNTIL THE NEXT TIDE

THE EVOLUTION OF
A SALTY DAWG

Jamie Golden

Haverhill House Publishing LLC

Until the Next Tide: The Evolution of a Salty Dawg
Black and White Edition
© 2025 Jamie Golden

Cover design & setup (to come) © 2025 Errick Nunnally
Cover photo © 2024 Eileen Counihan

ISBN 978-1-949140-61-3

First Edition

For more information, address:

Haverhill House Publishing LLC
643 E Broadway
Haverhill MA 01830-2420

Visit us on the web at www.haverhillhouse.com

UNTIL THE NEXT TIDE

THE EVOLUTION OF A SALTY DAWG

"These are my times when I'm at church, for there can be no heaven that can top that which is revealed through the sea."

For Shannon...
You are the sea beneath my fins.

And in memory of my mother.
Thanks for making us go outside.

Prologue

A Fishing Fool is Born

Vando Paolini. That was his name. I'm not sure how old I was when Vando took my little brother and me fishing—maybe nine or ten— but something stuck with me that day, and it wasn't just a rusty hook. I am thankful for that something every time I smell the salt in the air or hear the cries of frantic terns. This was our first real venture to the sea, to try our luck for the fish that prowled the depths. The excitement was un-containable, with the sights and sounds of nature surrounding us. The black-capped pirates twirled and dove, searching the surf for that lonesome sand eel, those that strayed just a feather too close to the ocean's surface. We watched for nervous water, where the surface might be about to explode with baitfish being ravaged by unseen predators from below. I loved every minute of that day. And so it began, on that little T-shaped pier just north of Boston, off Route One in Lynn, Massachusetts, surrounded by auto dealerships and strip joints, a young boy found himself hand-lining flounder, two at a time…and a fishing fool was born.

Vando was an old family friend, a short Italian guy who lived with his wife and children in downtown Framingham. I don't remember much about him, only glimpsed memories—his stature, his house, the smell of meatballs and sauce that Mrs. Paolini would cook inside their little Italian kitchen, the laundry billowing in the breeze on the old clothesline outside. You know, the kind—it looked like a giant, old-fashioned TV antenna and would spin when the wind picked up. Those are the only impressions that remain, except from one particular day. On that day, Vando, the kind of family friend that seems a rarity these days, offered to take my brother and me fishing. We were going for flounder, dropping our lines from the planks of a creaky pier that jutted into the inlet where the bay fed into the Atlantic. It wasn't the most exotic saltwater destination, under the shadow of Boston, but it was the sea, nonetheless. This wasn't fishing for sunfish, catfish, or perch; we were going for flounder. Winter Flounder, Summer Flounder, we didn't care and didn't know there was a difference. We were catching fish that would end up rolled in breadcrumbs and served with lemon. We were learning that fishing is self-sufficiency at its best.

We had our spots picked out along the railings, staking claim to our little corners that connected us to the undersea world. With eyes wide and rain slickers pulled tight, we watched closely as Vando gave us a lesson in baiting our wooden hand-lines, how to hook the clams, and how to work the rig towards the bottom. At the end of the braided line was tied an old coat hanger, the kind that had a little tube of cardboard attached from one end to the other. Vando had removed the tube, and at each end, he had tied a mono leader with a snelled hook. He had some lead attached to weight it against the current, and after baiting up with some clams, we lowered our lines towards the bottom.

Well, it wasn't long before the tide started dropping, and we were pulling healthy flounder onto the pier two at a time. A true Norman Rockwell moment, a couple of salty kids in yellow slickers, grinning from ear to ear, with a five-gallon bucket loaded with fresh flounder— and we caught them ourselves!

That did it! I was bitten and hooked. I was a fisherman.

But this book is about more than just fish tales. It is a journey through the swamps, the sand, the sea, and the foam. To faraway lands and some just a stone's throw away, with soggy sneakers, leaky waders, beach bums, and bathing beauties, and other adventures of the salty kind.

Good tidings, my friends.

Chapter 1

A Sweetwater Intro

Before I can dive deep into the salty world, I need to spend some time delving into the murky realm of sweetwater dreams; a place where the fishing bug really is nothing more than an ever-growing curiosity of what lurks beneath the shimmering reflection of sky. For some of us, that bug morphs into a little creek, gently sloping through twists and turns, over pebbles, around boulders, barely making a dent in the landscape. Maybe a slight undercut, hidden in shadows of wild grasses and thorny branches. A breeze, perhaps just a bit too strong, wrestles a grasshopper from its lone blade. It lands with barely a ripple, struggling to escape the waterworld it now finds as its unwanted vehicle.

From above, our eyes would watch it fade into the distance, a seemingly harmless ride on such a calm trickle of water. But then the rains come, and that little green insect is in for one hell of a ride. That fishing bug is now a full-fledged fever. That trickle is now a raging torrent, ripping at the walls of the muddy banks, dragging those thorny branches with it, and barreling over the once peaceful landscape, giving that little bug the ride of his life and dumping him into an over-flowing world. A farm pond, a lake, or perhaps a river. Yet, some of us grow into the fever. But first, I had to be the bug. In a place where the water isn't so blue. This water was more like a sweet tea, in a variety of colors from almost tap-water clear, to that of a deep rust. Where thorny branches, leaves, and whatever else took the ride to the bottom, slowly disintegrate, adding to the freshwater brew that is known throughout the angling community as…Sweetwater.

I'd wager that most kids first soaked a line in a little bucket of tea before dipping their toes in big blue; although if you were one of those lucky kids that grew up on the beach, or maybe a cherrystone's throw away, then you had a jump on us inlanders. Either way, that worked out just fine for me. One might think growing up in the western suburbs of Boston, just out of reach of the shadows of the big city, that the opportunities would be slim; but surprisingly, the mini-cities, mill towns, and sleepy villages hid many secrets from the concrete walls of Beantown. Wide lakes and reservoirs, beautiful little ponds, and wooded creeks and trickling streams offered numerous opportunities to the explorer. I could wax poetic of the colors of a picturesque New England backdrop, ablaze in the fire of Autumn, and it would be nothing but the truth. The region truly is magnificent, in all the vibrant shades of an artist's palette, although I think most of us New Englanders take it for granted. Maybe it's just that Autumn also signifies that soon another grey season is approaching, where we are only left with snow and cold for months on end, until the Robins return, and the buds show red on limbs anxious for green.

By the time I was in my late teens, my fishing skills were becoming more and more attuned to the fascinations of those I'd been reading about in fishing magazines. The main quarry of the majority of the angling world was the Largemouth Bass. Our favorite local spot, "the Res" (for reservoir), had easily given up the majority of its secrets regarding the Bigmouth, but I soon discovered that it held certain hideaways that were home to super-charged Smallmouth Bass.

I should note that we actually stumbled upon these secret locales while occasionally toting a cooler full of cold ones, trying to pass the time. I don't know what it is, but beer and fishing just seem to go together like the New England Patriots and Super Bowls. The reason I even mention this is that if a couple of pie-eyed kids can uncover smoking-hot fishing spots, anybody can, with a little effort. I can only imagine what kind of fish we would've been landing if we were working the shores without the IGLOO. I generally frown upon spot-burners, but I'm going to let some fly here and there, although I may be a bit more vague when I get to the Salt (for those who don't know, spot-burning is when some overly excited newcomer reveals a fishing spot, in a public way, like posting a picture on the Internet of a lesser known spot with an angler holding up a trophy fish, giving away its location). I won't tell you how to get there; but if you can figure them out on your own, good luck. Anyway, let's go fishing…

John Rice and Mike Moynahan have been my friends since we were kids. We grew up fishing the Sudbury Reservoir watershed, which covers parts of Framingham, Southborough, and Marlborough, Massachusetts. Most of our efforts were concentrated in the off-limits sections of Southborough, working the points, sandy coves, and deadwood found scattered along the shoreline, and we considered ourselves more or less experts when it came to finding the fish. Of course there were largemouth to be had in the expected areas, but when we started catching smallmouth, we changed our tactics a bit, and started focusing on them. If anyone has caught a Smallie before, you'll know why. Although largemouths grow considerably larger in most crossover locations, smallmouth will out-battle them on any given day. To steal an oft-repeated phrase, pound for pound, they fight like no other freshwater fish. An adrenalin charged, bronze-colored bulldog of a fish, they'll put your tackle to the test, tail-walking across the water like Bobby Orr charging the net.

The Route 30 dam, tucked away from the road in Southborough, has a gently sloping rock wall on the reservoir side that attracts some impressive Smallmouth Bass. When John, Mike, and I fished the dam back in the day, it was a place that was—while technically off-limits per the "No Trespassing" signs—free to explore, as there was really no security to worry about. There were a few occasions when we had to high-tail it out of there, with the local cops in less-than-hot pursuit, but for the most part it was ours, and ours alone.

It was the type of place you'd expect to see in a coming-of-age movie, where kids gathered during the day to jump off the pumphouse into the chilly waters, or built rafts to venture out on the high seas. But when the sun got low in the sky, and the mosquitoes started filling the air, it became something else. Oh, the magic of the black jitterbug. When we first discovered the fish-catching ability of this famous lure of our grandfathers, man did that raise the heart rate. As twilight rippled off the surface, we'd spread out along the shore, casting the cup-faced j'bug to the gentle surface, and wait for the landing rings to disappear and melt back into the greying waters. A slight snap and steady retrieve would signal the pop, pop, pop dance of the lure, creating a hypnotic wake atop the glassy, darkening surface. That serenity would only be interrupted by a topwater explosion, as a hungry bass would erupt from below. Sometimes a green back would reveal itself with a couple of jumps, giving away its identity as a largemouth. Other times, there was no mistaking the bronze fighter on the end of the line, as one jump was followed by an ongoing aerial display, followed by another, and another. It was under the veil of fading sunlight, and into the coming night, that the true pigs would emerge. Most sweetwater fishermen know that an approaching front, a change in the weather, followed by high barometric pressure, and what the average person would see as a bluebird day, always puts the fish on the feed. Now, if you can hit your favorite spot just prior to the front moving through, this should really increase your chances for a memorable outing. One such outing occurred on the banks of the Res, as the sun was sinking, and the distant sky rumbled with thunder.

The air crackled as we spied the impending storm, still quite a ways off, but coming on, ominous and angry. John opted for the trusty jitterbug, while I reached for my other go-to lure, a quarter-ounce, black-and-blue spinnerbait with a single Colorado blade. I had been having incredible success with the spinnerbait, and actually doubled up on the skirt so it would slow the fall rate; and the smallmouth had been crushing it. John had already scored on a nice largemouth in the three pound range, doing the jitterbug over a submerged weed bed in the corner of the dam, where the rocks took a hard turn down the shoreline. I climbed my way down the aqueduct, about a third of the way towards the pumphouse, and let rip a cast parallel to the rocks and about ten yards out. I worked the lure low and slow, trying to keep it near the bottom without hanging, when a massive hook-up had my rod arched and rocking. In a fraction of a second, a huge smallmouth took skyward, tail-walking frantically, as lightning flashed in the distance.

John had taken up alongside me, anxious to see the fish, and yelling "don't lose 'em!" Minutes passed while I worked to get the fish in close, until finally, I lipped a whopper, a twenty-four inch Smallie. A long, banded gold trophy. I don't really know the weight, but easily over four pounds, and a super catch for the MetroWest reservoir. But what really made this trip so special was that we weren't done yet. The storm seemed to stall over the distant hills, but assuming it was only a matter of time, we treated each cast as the last one before we'd have to make a quick exit. And the fishing took off. Every cast had at least a bump, if not a hook-up, including another smallmouth (twenty inches), and a largemouth nearing five pounds. It turned into a twenty-minute frenzy, with both species going on an epic bite, all while the lightning approached and the roar of thunder encroached. Stupid kids, we were, but fanatic anglers.

This is the place where I have to warn against such reckless behavior, risking electrocution. And stupid it was, but most teenagers will never claim to be smart. The point is, if the weatherman calls for an approaching front, get to your fishing hole, but keep an eye on the sky.

Chapter 2

Wheels and Waterways

Sweet sixteen. Or maybe I should call it *sweetwater* sixteen. Most teenagers look forward to a certain rite of passage when they hit this milestone birthday, for it signals another step in one's evolution towards independence. This is a time of anxiety and long lines at the Registry of Motor Vehicles. A time when a parent nervously hands the car keys to a wide-eyed kid with a learner's permit in his hand, and assumes the passenger role. Of course, this is eventually followed up by a flimsy piece of plastic, emblazoned with a picture of said kid, shit-eatin' grin from cheek to cheek. Freedom in the form of a shiny, new driver's license.

In the early 80's, this freedom took many routes. Sometimes it made right turns, like into the parking lot at Marian High School, in downtown Framingham, Massachusetts. Sometimes it made other turns. House parties, concert parking lots, and other questionable locales, like the McDonald's in Natick, which was a short walk through the woods to cross-town keg parties. Or maybe it was parked outside the Pizza Pub on Route Nine in Framingham, for Sunday evening blues Jam. The drinking age was eighteen in those days, and if you played it cool, the bouncers would let you slip on by if you were only shy by a matter of months. Yes, a few of these places weren't the kind that would make Mom and Dad proud, but we made it home in one piece.

Now, this shouldn't be seen as condoning drinking and driving, but these were different times. Stupid, care-free kids, less educated than in today's world. In those days, you wouldn't get much more than a slap on the wrist. The police would pull you over and make you dump your beers out. Either that, or they'd have you put them in the cruiser's trunk, before giving you a verbal kick in the ass, and telling you to get right home. It wasn't smart then, and it's just as dumb and dangerous today, but somehow we made it through.

Right turns, left turns, and wrong turns, yes, but those weren't the only turns that old car would make. That road sometimes led to adventures only the outdoors can provide. Fresh air instead of stale beer. When that steering wheel guided us into unexplored territory, all the wrong turns faded away and a new world awaited. Having wheels led to locales with exotic names like Wachusett and Quabbin, and exotic species like Lake Trout and Landlocked Salmon. With the wheels, came the waterways.

Rubber, meet blacktop. With my driver's license officially wearing away in my old, leather wallet (actually, I think it may have been tucked away in a Harley Davidson wallet, complete with chain, partly due to a little movie called "Easy Rider"), it was time to explore beyond our neighborhood fishing holes, as good as they might have been. These mid-to-late teen years were full of freedom and adventure, with fishing as the icing on the cake, at least initially. There were summer excursions to remote and beautiful rivers, clean and natural ribbons that carved their way through the western part of the state, the Berkshire mountains hiding their secrets. Rivers with names like the Deerfield or Westfield. Creeks and tributaries flowing with life. Those waters held big rainbows, bruiser browns, and native brookies.

We were mere explorers and amateur anglers, not schooled in the art of fly fishing, for which these rivers are held in high regard. Catch and release? Maybe. We didn't think about it much. We were just a bunch of kids with spinning rods, split shot, nightcrawlers, and a handful of spinners—Panther Martins, Roostertails, Blue Fox spinners, and maybe some small, balsa swimming plugs. That was all we needed, and that was all we brought, except for maybe some beef jerky, and a couple of six packs of Budweiser buried in ice at the bottom of a cracked, Styrofoam cooler.

Sometimes, the canoe would get tossed on the roof of Gary Esper's old, school-bus yellow, Chevy van. That old van covered many miles, avoiding blue lights and trespassing signs; though for the most part, we made or own rules. One expedition found us searching for a camping spot late at night, peering through the darkness of the Mohawk trail, along Route Two in the northwest corner of the Massachusetts. The fishing had been good, with a few rainbows dressed and ready for the frying pan, but we had no idea where we were. GPS? Nope, we're talking the early 80's. Maps? Shit no. We were adventurers. The "Question Authority" bumper sticker gracing the bumble bee van said it all. So, what was a group of wayfaring anglers to do? Why, pull over on the side of the road and set up camp, tent and all. Yup, right alongside Massachusetts State highway Route Two. We were the real fisher kings!

As you can imagine, the idea of a group of kids camping on the side of road ended up being as ridiculous as it sounds, or looked, and was most certainly not overlooked by the State Police trooper who happened by in the wee hours of the morning. Footsteps crunching, flashlight waving, and a stern request to vacate the tent, had us face to face with a less-than-amused cop. But all was not lost. As the man with the badge took the names "Gary Esper," "John Rice," and "James Golden" back to the cruiser to run a check on our status as upstanding citizens, he turned and asked a question. One that all fishing fools love to hear, when underage with a cooler of beer, and a tent on the side of a major roadway, albeit tucked away in the shadows of the Berkshires. This question opens the door to bond with the good Sheriff, and it went simply like this: "How's the fishing?"

There it was. That was the opening. And from there, we were all set. The man was a fisherman. And after exchanging fish tales, and getting a semi-lecture on how what we were doing was definitely heading towards one of those aforementioned *wrong turns*, he was on his way. I'd wager you wouldn't see a cop these days letting us stay roadside until sunup, but that was exactly what happened. We weren't saints, but we were never out looking to cause trouble. Just some young guys who wanted to see what was out there. But I won't say our sweetwater excursions didn't land us in hot water from time to time.

Gambling with the outlaw fishing attitude only works if you draw the right cards. When you do end up with a winning hand, you can skate by on luck, like the encounter on the Mohawk trail or the time we were coming back from a trip, canoe on the roof and cold beers in hand. Not exactly what you'd call *wicked smaht,* but let's just say "wisdom doesn't always come with age, it comes with learning from your mistakes."

On this sunny afternoon, Gary must've been holding a Royal Flush. When the blue lights came on behind us, we figured it was a traffic violation. To this day, I'm not really sure why we got pulled over. No turn signal? Stop sign? Regardless, we weren't drunk. No way near it from what I recall, but still, an open beer wasn't going to fly with the cop easing up to our bumper, or was it? Of course, an open container was illegal, but that lucky hand had other plans for us. In one swift and secret motion, Gary tossed his bottle over his shoulder, towards the back of the van, which was cluttered with, you guessed it, fishing stuff. The mirrored shades of the officer reflected into the van while driver and cop exchanged formalities, a ticket was rewarded to the card holder, and off we went. Back at the house, we opened the back of the van. There, glistening in the sun and looking like the bottle cap had just been pried from neck, an ice cold beer stood at attention with nary a drop spilled. That lucky hand had bought Gary a perfect toss, a ten point upright landing.

But the cards were changing, and the hand would be shown upon a new venture, an introduction to one of the state's legendary waters: Wachusett Reservoir. The first trip to Wachusett Reservoir, aka the "chu," can only be described as a complete failure. We weren't even technically fishing the reservoir, but more the watershed area of the Quinapoxet River, which pours into the big body of water in the upper northwest section of Thomas Basin. The river can be quite good at times, and is also stocked which trout, but frankly, we didn't know any better. To this day, I can say we haven't spent a whole lot of time fishing this area, based on successes from other stretches.

On that first trip to the watershed, we based our destination on hearsay, with dreams of Lake Trout and Landlocked Salmon, or maybe a big, Brown Trout. But this being another day spent in the fog of youth, it was really another trip to explore with friends, and enjoy a couple of cold cervezas. On that day, we were dealt a pair of deuces.

Carrying our tackle and a cooler down to the riverside, just downstream from the pump-house, we paid little attention to the rules posted on twisted green signs marking the area. But we would soon know all about these signs. As a glistening rainbow lay atop the grassy bank, fresh from making a meal of a blue fox spinner, one of the guys spotted the environmental officer on the opposite side of the river, spyglasses pointed directly at us. After stowing the binoculars in his truck, and a short hop across the bridge, we were on the wrong side of a heated lecture. The "green cop" didn't let us slide out of this one, but it could've been worse. I guess a pair of "twos" is better than no hand at all, and rather than arresting us on the spot, he notified us that we'd be receiving a summons to appear in Worcester court. We were told that only one of us had to appear, to represent our group of five: Gary Esper, John Rice, Mike Moynahan, Paul Kavanaugh, and myself. We elected our old friend, Paul, to face the judge, mostly because he was not following the sacred rule of public drinking in the forbidden zone, and had been going about his excesses freely, including flashing around a bottle of tequila. After ending up with a hefty fine, or what seemed hefty for a bunch of teenagers, it was time to retire this card game we were playing. Time to get serious. And time to take a serious look at this Wachusett fishery.

Chapter 3

The Wachusett Watershed

Before we hit the shores of this central Massachusetts hot spot, a little background on its origins. In the late 1890's, the rapid expansion of the Boston area revealed an inadequate water supply for the region. In 1897, a dam was constructed on the Nashua River in Clinton, MA. Shortly thereafter, six and half square miles, encompassing parts of the towns of West Boylston, Boylston, Sterling, and Clinton, were underwater, flooded by the new impoundment. The resulting reservoir and supporting aqueducts would serve the metropolitan Boston area as its primary water source until the larger Quabbin Reservoir was built in the 1930's.

While Quabbin is also considered a great spot for bay state anglers due to its proximity, we rarely ventured there, even though that reservoir allows small engine watercraft. In hindsight, we probably should've spent more time exploring its deep waters, but proximity being what it was, wayfaring the Wachusett shoreline was more attractive. The 'chu was just a bit over an hour's drive from Boston, and half that from our Framingham home base. And while the Quabbin appears as though it may have an advantage over its smaller sister res due to boat access, I'm not so sure. With the shoreline restrictions, overall, there is less fishing pressure. Sure, you have to work harder for a bite, but a look at the record books tells a story that only adds to the appeal of this sweetwater destination. With Lake Trout capable of reaching mammoth proportions, jumbo Smallmouth, Rainbow and Brown Trout, and silver-flanked Landlocked Salmon, anglers literally come out of the woodwork to rush to the sandy, pine-dotted shores.

Unlike most of the lakes and ponds of Massachusetts, the reservoir has a closed season, and thus an opening day (as does Quabbin). Typically the first Saturday in April, depending on ice-out, opening day has long been a tradition in these parts for Wachusett fishermen, and normally the shore will be scattered with anglers across all reaches. During these first days of Spring, the bite can be red-hot with rising warmer temps, spiking activity beneath the blue-grey ripples.

Lake Trout is the primary target, which in itself is a prize, as the reservoir is one of only a few locations in Southern New England where the largest of the trout species (actually a Char, but considered part of the family) can be caught. But lakers are surely not the only sport. As for the aforementioned state records, the 'chu can lay claim to Landlocked Salmon (10.2), Smallmouth Bass (8.2), Brown Trout (not abundant, but for the record 19.10), and the big momma of the group, Lake Trout, at 24lbs even (caught in 2004). An impressive list, and a true sweetwater paradise! It was a sea of dreams, where exotic species were waiting to tip the scales.

Our first serious excursion came after some local research and tackle-shop prying. This trip found me and the crew headed down a side road just off Route70 in Boylston. We had checked out topographical maps and marked gates where access would bring us close to deep water. As we made our way down the wooded side road, we were greeted by a sight that only fueled the fishing fever. Walking toward us was an older gentleman, a little grey in the whiskers and probably about my age as I write this twenty-five years later. There before us was one happy dude, a king of the sweetwater, wearing a grin that matched the fish he carried in each hand. In one was a smallmouth that looked to be topping five pounds. A true beast. In the other was Landlocked Salmon a bit smaller, but still quite a prize—a silver rocket. The funny thing is, when we threw accolades at him from the window, he said thanks, but still added that the laker bite was a bit slow. That lucky son of a bitch was towing two trophies back to his car, and still wanted more action on the big Lake Trout. Well, that had us scrambling out the doors, bait bucket sloshing, and dust in our wake. We were going to join the legends of the local tackle shop wall of fame before you knew it.

As you probably guessed, we didn't become stars at Wachusett Bait and Tackle that day; but we fared okay, with a steady pick of lakers from two to four pounds. Not bad for some bass fisherman from MetroWest. The days passed, and then a year or two, but the annual springtime excursions remained. The lakers got a bit bigger, on occasion, and the *smallies* and salmon made an appearance here and there. But the truly big fish were still out there. One crisp, early April morning, a few seasons removed from our first real outing, we settled on a popular spot off Route140 behind the West Boylston Fire Department.

The fire road along the res followed the shore towards a creek that dumped into a nice little cove. In the spring, this creek would see smelt making their way upstream to spawn. In those days, there was a great deal of smelt, and from what I've heard recently, there is now ridge smelt replacing the river species. A bigger species which could make for interesting, full-bellied specimens caught in the future. Well, this particular day saw us setting up just outside the bend to the cove, where this creek dumped in. We were geared up in the traditional laker style, common back in the day, with our spinning rods loaded with eight-pound mono, with an egg sinker atop a small swivel or split shot, followed by a leader with a lively medium-to-large shiner pinned to the hook on the end. Some guys prefer floating dead shiners off the bottom, but I always prefer live when possible. The shiners would be tossed out, bail left open, and a loop of line tucked under a rubber band, snug near the reel seat. Finally, a small square of tin foil was pinched on the line as it exited the rod tip. Yes, I know this wasn't the most eco-friendly set-up, and there are flags or bells that can be attached, but this was how we did it back in the day.

Anyways, it worked well, and you could be down the shoreline a bit and still see if you got a hit. How it works is when a laker or other fish would hit your bait, the line would pull free from the rubber band, and the tin foil would go shooting into the water. When this happened, you quickly tended to the rod, picked up the slack slowly, and when you felt pressure, set the hook. We went through this exercise a few times that day, with at least one five-pounder in the mix. Pretty decent day, or so we thought, until the guy a few trees down had a monster take a liking to his shiner. We saw him running towards his rod, just as the tin foil disappeared beneath the surface. The rod was shaking like it was electrified, bouncing in its makeshift rod holder, the dried out branch straining to give way. We watched with anticipation as he battled the brute, and before long he was dancing along the shore, his compadre ready with the net, which soon would scoop up a decorated laker, looking all of one hundred pounds.

I'm not sure why, but we've drifted away from fishing this spot in recent years, although it may have had something to do with my own battle with a monster on an icy morning a few years later. I can't recall if it was opening day, but it was surely around then, and an interesting one at that. The shoreline was well-crowded, and our usual spot along the point just before the cove had no open areas, or at least none we wanted to claim. I can't stand it when some mindless zombie parks his arse right on top of your designated port, and I didn't want to be that guy.

What added to the crowd was something not too seen around opening day. Ice! The main body of the reservoir had been open and free of ice, which is a prerequisite for the management to open it for the season. But this morning, a large sheet had drifted in close to shore, most likely from a floating mass further out in the reservoir. Well, the combination of the two obstacles pushed me up inside the cove, where the channel narrows, and eventually meets the outpouring of the creek. Overall, a decent spot, except for the slope of the bank, which was barely manageable by foot. Regardless, this was my spot.

I carefully rigged my two rod and reel combos, sent my shiners out for a swim, pinched the tin foil on the end, and settled into the waiting game. Moments passed, bait was changed up, and the wait continued as I headed downshore to chat up a couple of fellow anglers. A few minutes had passed when a glance towards my rods caught the tin foil from one rig quickly heading seaward. Kicking up dirt as I hustled towards my set-up, I grabbed the rod, felt the fish, and set into it hard.

Well, as hard as I could. See, one thing about this trip, to add to the ice, and the crowds, was this particular set-up was still sporting six pound mono from early spring trout fishing. This would be just fine for the average fish, but this was no average fish. This was a legit slob. I patiently and expertly fought the fish, letting it run, using the bend in the rod to tire the fish, when it finally came into view. What a fish! Rolling sideways, I'd gain some line, inching it closer, and now the runs that followed each lift of the rod were getting shorter, until at last it was right alongside the bank. Did I say this bank was brutal, the slope arcing into the deep channel? It was almost impossible to stand at the edge, and it soon became clear what I needed, and what I normally don't take fishing. A net! I yelled down the shore to the gents I was talking to earlier, and just as one of them snatched up his net and turned in my direction...pop! I could only watch as "the one that got away" got away. Of course, it wasn't the first, and certainly not the last, but damn, it never gets easy losing a monster fish.

I haven't spent a great deal of time fishing there in the Summer, but as storied as these waters may be, the pressure fades from the shores as the leaves lose their color and ghosts of the season past take up residence. Maybe it's the chill in the air, the warmth of a wood stove beckoning, or simply just resigning oneself to the couch, waiting for the lakes and ponds to freeze over. Perhaps hunting season is in your sights and you've shelved the fishing gear for the season. But, for you fellow anglers with the fishing affliction, the fish are hungry and on the move, and you should be too.

Baitfish like smelt can be seen swimming the edges and ridges. Landlocked Salmon will be heading to the rivers feeding the res, the urge to spawn pushing them onward. Lakers move into shallower waters as the water cools, and Rainbow Trout will be on the hunt for smelt. Brown Trout too, will be moving into the river mouths, seeking fresh salmon eggs, spilled forth from spawning salmon. I might even go as far to say Autumn is a better time to fish the reservoir, and not just for the fishing. Gone are those bullshit ticks of the spring, and all the possible diseases they bring. Here, especially in Springtime, stay more to the fire roads and paths. Last year, John Rice and I literally pulled twenty ticks each from our clothing, and my wife had to dig two out of my skin. Man, I hate those things. But, not so much in the fall. Also, no mosquitoes, and a fraction of the anglers of Spring. It really takes on a different feel, and the fishing picks up just as the Summer season and early Fall fishing, saltwater in particular, winds down.

Wachusett Reservoir's abundant Lake Trout

A couple of years ago, on a beautiful Fall morning, we arrived on the banks of the reservoir with steam rising from our coffee cups, the mist from each breath exhaled in swirls. The chill soon burnt off, as the warming sun rose over the pines, and the shadows collapsed. Initially, we were bound for one of our usual spring spots along the fire road that runs west of Route 140, a bit past where I lost the jumbo years before. We were hoping to exploit a spot that generally has higher water levels in the springtime, but come fall, is typically much lower, allowing access to often inaccessible areas. This little island in the spring, projecting off a shallow point, should now be a sandy peninsula, offering access to a deeper drop-off than some of the surrounding shoreline. This would open up the water column for shorebound anglers like us, increasing our odds at intercepting hungry lakers.

As luck would have it, rain from earlier in the week had the water running high, as witnessed through binoculars spied through from the causeway parking lot. Time for Plan B. What's Plan B, you might ask? Hell, I don't know. We were making it up as we went along. We decided to explore an area we hadn't previously spent much time fishing. It was back to the deep ridges off Route 70. This was the aforementioned *tick city* in the springtime, so we checked the map for points and creeks before wandering aimlessly, and settled on a spot near a small flow, where a deep cove quickly narrows. The hope was that baitfish would be trapped inside the *valley*, and hungry lakers would be stalking them.

We set out four rods, two relatively deep with medium shiners on the bottom, and one along the shallower ledges. I began fan-casting and working different water levels, bouncing bottom, jigging mid-depth, and swimming shallow, with my half-ounce perch Kastmaster going untouched. After exhausting the Kastmaster, I was in the middle of changing over to a rainbow crocodile spoon when I saw line peeling off my spinning outfit with a deep shiner. I dropped the lure rod and grabbed the bait rod, tightened the drag, and waited for the line to come tight. Rearing back I knew I had stuck a good fish, a really good fish! The fish, which I assumed was a laker, was solidly hooked and ripping drag—but I knew I had her.

Big mistake.

I could feel the fish diving and felt something just as the line parted. The rough cliffs to our right carried downward, their sharp edges a hidden disaster. Shortly after, I had a follow-up run, only to fall victim to the same unseen rocks. The fish were there, but we couldn't catch them. Plan B needed some fine tuning. We decided to move up in the cove a bit further, less rocks, but shallower. The action was not what you would call fast and furious, with just one short run after nearly an hour and a half of fish-tales.

It was time for Plan C, which was really just a return to Plan A. While the water levels were higher than we'd hoped for, we decided to pack up and move to our springtime spot, or at least in the general vicinity. Setting up on one of the high-banked points, our decision to move was rewarded in a matter of minutes. At first, it seemed more an illusion than reality, as both rods were hit almost simultaneously, pinched tin foil racing and disappearing below the grey surface. A dual battle was soon to follow, complete with the bulldogging determination of a couple of cookie-cutter forktails. After a quick release, we watched the lakers swim back to their dark home-waters.

No sooner had the ripples subsided, when the buzz from the other bait rod started singing.

John worked this fish, one of similar size, to the sand. The action slowed after that last forktail, as the shadows grew longer, and daylight began to fade. The late afternoon chill was cloaking the hillside as we began the "just five more minutes" countdown, when an unexpected visitor took interest in a shiner we had set out under a bobber. The red and white plastic ball disappeared in a flash, and didn't come back up. The surprise took on an added twist when, not a Landlocked Salmon, but the purple sides of a beautiful eighteen-inch Rainbow Trout came into view. The last rainbow of the year. It just goes to show that sometimes, the first plan is the best plan, even when it doesn't look perfect. Though, one of these days, I do plan to return to the sharp edges of "Plan B" armed with heavy artillery!

While the main reservoir can provide outstanding fishing, I would be remiss if I didn't tell you about the creeks and tributaries feeding into the big body. At times they can provide some damn good fishing, and at the very least, a chance to explore the wilds surrounding the reservoir.

Actually, one of my favorite things about fishing these creeks and slight rivers is the location, and the beauty that surrounds them. Pine trees, some scarred with the determination of the local beaver population, teetering as a giant spindle waiting to fall. Others have already succumbed to the toothy, and some say bothersome, rodents, and now leave a patchwork of obstacles along and across the flowing brooks. I don't give much thought to the beavers, although they can kill a creek, or produce a pond where trout congregate. So are they pests or a sign of a healthy local ecosystem? Depending on my objective, I might vote one way or the other.

The trees that remain majestic have given me glimpses of bald eagles, osprey, and various hawks. One of the first creeks I happened upon came as a result of premature cabin fever, or maybe just a fishing fool not ready to give up for the season. On that chilly December morning, driven more by the idea of simply getting outside than the thought of actually catching anything, I threw my trout gear in the truck and made the drive out towards the Wachusett Reservoir, map book in hand. I knew there were native brookies, as well as holdovers in the tributaries, so I decided to give it a shot.

After pulling over opposite the old stone church, a famous landmark in West Boylston, which hugs the reservoir, I flipped through the pages of the map, analyzing the creeks and rivers feeding into and out of the big body of water, and noticed the little brook off Manning Street in Holden. Weaving my way along the backroads, I eventually came across a small dirt and gravel lot. A sign posted on the opposite side of the road stated I was at Trout Brook Reservation. There were no other cars present on a frosty December morning, and I was probably nuts for being out there. Not exactly the conditions I would've preferred. But under a bright sun, with the hawks soaring overhead and the smell of pine in the air, just being outside with the crispness in your lungs can make you forget about the cold trying to creep in through every loose button. I wasn't quite sure what to expect from this unexplored territory. Maybe it was worked over a thousand times, or perhaps just a path for dogwalkers. But, as I made my way along the path, and the rippling and tumbling sound of the creek rang through the brush, I began to think differently. It felt different. So close to civilization, but far away at the same time, and not the place for local soccer moms to take Fido for a run.

After a brief trek, I came across what can only be described as a perfect pool, obvious to the eye as one that *should* get worked over quite frequently in the high season. This was definitely a regular stop. But today, with Jack Frost nipping at my toes, I had this little hole to myself. And yes, welcoming trout reflecting through the ripples. Standing atop the embankment that overlooks the pool, Brook Trout were plainly visible, their flanks ablaze with purple and orange colors so vivid I could pick and choose where to cast my bait. Not being much of a fly fisherman, my tackle included small spinners and spoons, but on this day I drifted a small piece of night crawler, attached to a tiny hook about eighteen inches below a small split shot. I wanted my bait drifting and bouncing in the current, casting upstream and rolling into the waiting fish. And on this day, the little brookies were more than willing to have a taste.

For the next two hours or so, I hooked up regularly, under pristine conditions, bouncing from pool to riffle to pool. Other trips to Trout Brook revealed similar results, with one in particular that stands out not for the trout, but for another angler who put the squeeze on us. John and I headed out on another end of season trip, with the intention of repeating previous visits with hungry brookies. We covertly scouted the pool and neighboring riffles, and sure enough, trout were visible, with their spawning colors giving them away in an occasional flash. A snicker and a grin framed the confidence we had, knowing the pool was ours, and again, the late season saw no other fishermen as competition.

Ah yes, but the fool's eye only sees what is right in front of him. A few casts in without a hit, a bump, or a sniff was about as normal as Peter Boyle's *abby normal* brain in "Young Frankenstein," and the trout were pooled up, when the monster appeared. Okay, not a monster, but a furry, little bastahd (for us proper Bostonians) bobbing in the middle of the pool, holding a freshly caught brookie between its paws, and gnawing away at the tasty treat. An otter had taken a liking to our fishing hole, and there wasn't a whole lot we could do about. I suppose I might've cracked a smile while being schooled in the fine art of fishing while the animal rolled and played, catching fish with ease. But that's the Wachusett watershed for you. I must note that my last visit a few years back saw no fish in the pool. Bad timing? Conditions? I'm planning to follow up in the coming seasons, and hope it hasn't fallen off like so many others, due to human encroachment. Maybe there was just another hungry otter that day.

Naturally, from the first venture into the tributaries of the watershed, we soon explored the other creeks and rivers (if you can call them that), that feed the reservoir. One of the better known areas is the Quinapoxet River, which is not far from Trout Brook, and is actually a feeder to that brook. The upper reaches of the "Quinnie" have a population of native Brook Trout, along with holdover Rainbows and Browns, and can produce straight through the winter, if you're willing to brave the chilly temps and a few snowflakes. These days that shit just ain't for me, but once upon a time I would have braved the frigid winters to soak my bones along this slip n' slide. There are big fish living there, particularly below the pumphouse, where the river pours from a dam, pooling in the Quinapoxet Basin from the upper river and dumping into the Thomas Basin area in the northwest corner of the res.

Honestly, we haven't done a great deal of fishing in that area, other than the time we got popped by the rangers while drinking beers tossing worms, but I know there are big fish in residence. I've recently seen repeated reports from the sharpies who fish this area in the fall, revealing a monster Brown Trout fishery. The big browns have seemingly been a mystery in years past, but I'm starting to believe this was a matter of anglers not targeting them. I've got these big bruisers, fish over five pounds, moving up on my local target list for late fall, and time will tell if I can figure them out.

The tributary that I prefer, for a variety of reasons, is the Stillwater River. While the salmon fishery in the Quinnie River is more of a folk tale these days due to the dam downstream, the Stillwater is well-known for its autumn run of Landlocked Salmon. A beautiful, free-flowing river, it is one of the only locations in Massachusetts where a spawning run exists for the native population of Landlocked Salmon. As the temperatures drop in the early fall, the salmon leave the safety of the cool depths of Wachusett Reservoir, and make their way to the northern reaches of the res through the basin and up into the tributary. Although not very big as rivers go, the Stillwater has structure, holes, twists and turns, and clear water…conditions that are a rare find just a short drive from Boston.

As with my introduction to Trout Brook, my discovery of the Stillwater came by way of exploration, a sunny day in early October when I spied the river through the multi-colored leaves. I knew I had found something special. And—forgive me if I repeat myself over and over as you flip the pages—get a map book, study it, keep it safe. You'll find more bends in the river and hidden coves by simply tossing an eyeball on a map. That first trip to the Stillwater, the all-seeing eye had me crossing the Muddy Pond Road. bridge, somewhere along the West Boylston/Sterling town line. Just over the bridge, I pulled my truck to the side, and rumbled to a dusty stop in a makeshift dirt lot. At first glance, the river looked nothing like what could be seen between the pines during my drive. At the railing, it appeared to be a slow, dark, meandering flow, maybe thirty feet across. But glance in either direction, north or south, and the river comes alive and reveals itself as more into a creek, with pebbles, holes, undercuts, and tumbling water.

I was on a stealth mission for this one, flying solo, and after gathering my gear, I made my way discreetly through the brush along the river. Some people might think it's nuts, but throwing your shadow over waiting fish will spook them sure enough, even before you spot them. Giving the bridge a quick look, I decided to work my way downstream, tossing my bait under the embankments and in the riffles, eventually coming to a stretch where the river twists and turns. This would seem to be tight quarters to flyfish, but fortunately I'm not a fly guy and my light tackle was perfectly suited for what I was looking for.

I had a small box of Panther Martin spinners, but I opted for a snip of nightcrawler, approximately fourteen inches below a small split shot. The split shot was ticking just off the bottom, zipping in the current under the opposite side embankment, and dropping into the undercut, when my line came tight. A slight snap of the wrist, and I was fast to a nice fish. I was surprised, expecting to connect with small, native brookies, akin to those swimming over at Trout Brook Reservation. I had something much better on the line. A Rainbow, or perhaps a decent Brown Trout? And then there it was. A silver bolt of lightning, making repeated jumps in the fast water, testing the light monofilament in the current, and moments later, a striking nineteen inch salmon lay on the bank. Now that's an introduction. I wouldn't catch any more salmon that day, but the few brookies that followed kept the smile on my face.

An occasional salmon would find the hook over the next few years, as we explored the river into more remote areas—places where beavers left their mark, and pencil-stubbed pine trees. But more and more in the following years, my boots found their way to terrain filled with sand, with salt in the air. Even so, I would never be completely done with Wachusett. It had too much to offer to leave it alone. Still, years passed, big fish were caught, and big fish were lost, and one day, just like that, I picked up the pen, putting words to paper.

Okay, it was a computer keyboard, but just like that, I was a contributing writer to a couple of the region's exceptional fishing magazines. Driven by journalistic inquiries, one day, many years after my last trip to the Stillwater, I decided it was time to return. I had a piece in mind for "The Fisherman" highlighting the reservoir's tributaries, and I needed to get out and do some research. Almost two decades after my last visit, I wanted to see for myself if the river was still alive. I followed the same route I first set out on, feeling like Lewis and Clark retracing their steps. Faded memories came back to me. I carried essentially the same gear with me, although with years of surfcasting under my belt, I now approached the scene with lightweight waders, and it was a damn good thing too.

One thing I want to stress here is the abundance of ticks. These little bastards are everywhere in the Wachusett area, and the banks of the Stillwater are no exception. I've seen the pain they can cause, when my own sister suffered with Lyme disease for months until the antibiotics finally pushed it into dormancy. Waders won't protect you from them, but you'll see them a lot easier. I've had twenty-tick days, and let me tell you, it's no fun digging even one out, so get some tick spray, and cover up good.

Anyway, let's get back in the river. As always, sneaking up on the bank is the way to go, and like my first visit, and in the exact same undercut, a small piece of nightcrawler drifted under the bank. First cast. Well hello there, Mr. Landlocked. I'll be damned if a beautiful fifteen inch salmon hadn't graced me with its hunger, and followed in the footsteps of its ancestors. The rest of the day saw no more fish landed, outside of some micro-brookies and fingerlings, but I did enjoy watching five nice landlocks much larger than the one I landed ignore my offerings while relaxing in the shade of a river-spanning tree limb. As I sat back on the bank of the river, the day ended with a rare treat when a bald eagle soared overhead. For a writer, a few more fish might've added to the story, but for my fisherman's soul, I simply could not have planned it better.

I recently updated my sweetwater tales to include a little secret I've stumbled upon, that takes me back to the main body of the Wachusett Reservoir. In the past couple of years, always reluctant to wrap up my fishing season, the urge for one more cast found me on the shoreline in the waning weeks of November as turkey and football were more in mind than freezing fingertips. The salmon were nearing the end of their upriver spawning runs, but the weeks preceding were no doubt filled with the joys of the spawn, including tumbling salmon eggs. Now I don't know if the spawn is trickling down into the open waters of the reservoir, or whether the ridge smelt, which has become primary forage, is stacking up on the drop offs near the shallows, but regardless, hungry trout have been capping off the season. And not lakers, like most would suspect. Of course, this time of the year, there are nice Lake Trout hitting lures and bait, as well, but I'm talking about rainbows, and big fish to boot.

One recent Sunday morning John and I decided to brave the colder than normal temps, and go in search of big lakers. The clock was working against us, as the Patriots were on in a few hours. I know you haters outside of New England don't give two shits about the Pats, and I get it. I mean losing to them year after year.... Hell, I'd hate them, too. And then you had other NFL owners conspiring with the Commissioner to drum up some Deflategate nonsense. A puff of air which was undoubtedly caused by cold temps, now used to punish the greatest QB of all time, and for what? Delivering crushing defeats to these other teams for two decades. I guess to other NFL fans, the Pats felt like the New York Yankees of my youth, always destroying the Red Sox dreams, and therefore becoming the evil empire. Regardless, Tom Brady and Belichick will always be the greatest of all time, and I'm not just being wicked *smaht*. They made Patriots football must watch TV, so John and I were going all in during the few hours before gametime.

We had heard that the bite was decent along Route 70, from Gate 14 to 8, but with our limited time before kick-off, we opted for the power lines near the causeway. The funny thing about this place is that anglers sometimes avoid this area because they *think* it will be crowded, which results in light pressure or none whatsoever. Perhaps that was the case on that day, but I think freezing temps had something to do with it.

With the plan in motion, we grabbed some shiners from B&A Tackle, just up the road, and set up under the powerlines. Alternating between shiners on the bottom and under a float, and Kastmaster spoons, we plied the water column close to the main road. A couple of nice lakers found our shiners down deep, but nothing was taking an interest in the shallow baits. A bit of a drought followed the initial action, so with my mind on the clock, I changed tactics sooner than later. I decided to drop some powerbait down deep, while we tossed Kastmasters, and kept one shiner on the bottom. Small salmon soon broke the deep freeze we were stuck in, but not enough to be worth the frozen fingertips.

And then...you know that moment in the back of your head when you begin to contemplate heading for the barn? Well, that moment was here, except for one glitch in my peripheral vision. Out of the corner of my eye, I caught the rod tip bounce on the powerbait rod, and as I rushed to grab it, the reel, with drag loosened, started buzzing. In one motion, I grabbed the rod, palmed the spool, set the hook and tightened the drag to its fighting weight. I knew immediately this was not a small salmon, nor a laker. It fought hard, down dirty hard, and made a few rushes to the surface without ever breaking it. I suspected big trout, but when I first saw color, it radiated silver, and I thought nice salmon. Minutes later, sweating even though ice was forming on my beard, I saw the fish a bit closer this time. Silver yes, but fat, and a beautiful red hue running its flanks, topped with a touch of olive. A healthy, five pound rainbow couldn't wait until Christmas to break out the holiday colors.

With this fish onshore, I could finally get my adrenaline down, snap a few pics, and gently release the fish for another day. Later that day, while watching the Pats dismantle another team, we made plans to get back to those rainbows the coming Thanksgiving week. But when the time came, John opted for the warmth inside his house, so I made the jaunt alone. With the reservoir closing on the last day on the month, even a steady snowfall couldn't keep me from at least tossing metal. My dedication paid off with two more beautiful Rainbow Trout, twenty and twenty-two inches, the latter fish easily three pounds. With a record-breaking winter on tap, it certainly wasn't a bad way to wrap up the sweetwater season. And the cherry on top? Well, that would come in early February, with Malcolm Butler's end-zone interception of the Seattle Seahawks, sealing the victory and giving Tom Brady and the New England Patriots their fourth Super Bowl Championship.

Chapter 4

Salt Transfusion

Ladies and gentlemen, it's time to roll back the clock and take a ride to the mid-1980s, when the sweetwater in my veins was transfused with a salty brine. The origin of this transfusion had its adolescent roots closer to home, when the days melted into yesterdays, and rock n' roll and pretty girls took precedence. As a kid with only occasional trips and family outings to the beach, I didn't have the exposure to the saltwater fishing I would come to love until I was captain of my own ship, or at least until I had a driver's license—but the beach was always there. There were many days when Mom would load up the station wagon, siblings, friends, coolers, and hit the road bound for the north shore or Cape Cod. Coca cola, comic books, frisbees, snorkeling, and even homemade spears for flounder would round out the day, but not much fishing. I'm sure there were days when the Bluefish were just off the beach and I didn't know it. Maybe even a schoolie Striped Bass, although these were lean years for the bass, and mostly they were scarce.

Of course, I didn't know any of that at the time. No, we were preoccupied with what most adolescent boys are at the beach. If we were lucky enough, my Dad would give my brother and me a sign it was time to take a walk along the water. Often we found ourselves at

Ogunquit Beach, in southern Maine, which my folks had recently discovered was one of the most beautiful beaches in all of New England. It also had Canadian tourists. Now, you may ask what would get us all excited about that? Well, let's just say the "free the nipple" campaign was never an issue with the girls from Quebec. And so it was, that my father, brother, and I would don our sunglasses and make the trek towards boob beach, knocker highway, as it were.

As eye-popping as that was, it wasn't always about the curves of the fairer sex. Occasionally we'd venture to other nearby locales, including the dock to see the boats unload their catch before hitting the lobster shack. Dad managed to get us on an occasional trip offshore on one of the Party Boats in Perkins Cove, plying the depths for Cod and Haddock. Looking back, I didn't appreciate it much at the time, but I sure miss those days now and then. He wasn't around much when we were kids, always sparring with my mother, eventually separating, and then succumbing to cancer in 1987. Although his later years saw him and all of us grow much closer, it was as if he didn't quite know how to be a family man until he had some years in the rearview mirror. But the good times certainly were good. It was easy, being with him.

My Dad was a fun guy. James Laurence Golden Jr., a former Massachusetts State Representative, complete with his cronies, and considered one of the "wild and crazy guys" of the 1970's political landscape. A fun guy, but not much of a fisherman. Now in most cases that wouldn't mean a whole lot, but we're talking about a guy who grew up in or around the water. Whether we're talking about sailing on the Mystic River as a kid, or serving in the Coast Guard on Kodiak Island, Alaska, the water was always a part of his life, but for whatever reason, that fishing fever that eventually takes hold of the true angling fanatics, never got its hooks into him. Sailing, yes. The love of the Sea, yes. But not fishing. This love of the sea not only existed within my father, but throughout the whole Golden family, with aunts and uncles, cousins and quahogs scattered from the Boston area to Gloucester, just a stone's throw away from the chilly, Cape Ann surf. A welcome retreat when the mercury boils, and the pavement bakes in "MetroWest" Boston. Good Harbor Beach, here we come!

It's amazing how the body reacts when that big toe first meets the Gloucester surf. I swear there's a half second delay before the rest of the body realizes what just happened, before every muscle in your body tenses and your teeth clench down. But, as ridiculous as it sounds, you do get used to it, and before you know it, you're bodysurfing right alongside other brave souls, foolhardy enough to ignore the temps in favor of a good swell. And then of course, you have Salt Island, just offshore Good Harbor Beach. I still have nightmares of the fire ants that live on the island. The funny thing about the island is you can only walk to it at low tide, and just barely, at least that's the way it was when we wide-eyed adventurers would make the trek. Unfortunately, I didn't discover the fire ants until my feet were covered up. But all thoughts of fire-ants would quickly disappear when we would settle in at my Uncle Richie's house, up the hill and overlooking Salt Island. With the lobster pot steaming under the ever-watchful eye of an enormous lobster mount (a taxidermist's masterpiece), us kids would be busy climbing the apple tree in the front yard, while the sounds of one of the adults tickling the ivory on the piano inside resonated through the leaves. And when the dinner bell rang, we all knew we were in for a treat. Lobster caught just off the beach, and around the rocks, with corn-on-the-cob to finish us off. I sometimes wonder whether the guy who created the "Life Is Good" corporation had come upon that idea while sitting over a plate of cracked claws and tails…

Then there was the summer I spent in Rockport, Massachusetts. As a fifteen year old kid who liked to live up to his namesake (see "wild and crazy guy"), my parents thought it would be a good idea to have me live and work at my Uncle Terry's inn. Not a particularly bad idea, since Terry and my Aunt Diane had recently purchased the Beach Knoll Inn, and needed help that first summer. Well, let's just say that I wasn't overly enthusiastic about the situation, being separated from my friends for a couple of months. I didn't properly appreciate the opportunity I had to explore the coves, and beaches. While the Inn was a fascinating place, with hidden passages and caves from colonial days conjuring images of pirates and smugglers, most of my days were filled with turning over rooms for eager tourists. But, on occasion, I did find my way down to the pier with a fishing rod in hand. Kicking back on that old concrete pier, a few yards short of the quaint shops of Bearskin Neck and every north shore artist's favorite subject, Motif No.1, a long-haired kid in cutoffs caught some of the most beautiful flounder and pollock. They weren't the biggest fish, and not really beautiful at all, but when I got back to the inn, my Aunt turned what I had just caught into some of the most delicious fish chowder to ever grace a potter's crock. And I caught it! Some days, life really is good, and would only get better. A few years later, my eyes were pointed south, to the sandy beaches of Cape Cod, and the salt would forever be instilled in my veins.

Chapter 5

Well I'm Southbound, Baby – Hello Cape Cod

I love the "Cape," as it is known locally. Don't me wrong: I love the ocean in all its glory, the brilliant blue water of the Florida Keys, the rocky shores of Maine, and all the beaches in between. But the Cape is special. As a kid growing up twenty-five miles inland, Cape Cod was a magical place. Whether it was a couple of weeks for summer break, or visiting my grandmother on Thanksgiving in Chatham or Sandwich, we'd wait anxiously in the back seat of the car, my sister, brother, and I angling to be first one to see and call out the bridge before the others.

Only sixty-five miles, the hour-long drive to the Sagamore Bridge might as well have been like driving to Miami (add a half hour of traffic, and it felt that far). But when we peered out the window crossing the famous Cape Cod Canal, looking down at the rippling water and sails highlighting the blue, all worries faded. The Cape represented nothing but good times for us kids. Catching eels in the grass along the banks of Little Pleasant Bay, just over the Chatham/Orleans border. Renting a sunfish to bounce in the waves off Harding's or Ridgevale Beach with Dad. Hot dogs, kites, 4th of July fireworks, seagulls and salt in the air. Cloudy days meant go-carts, or maybe a drive-in movie at night.

The fun only grew up slightly when the high school years arrived. Truckloads of friends, barreling down route 6 to beach fires, guitars, hidden beers in the dunes. Concerts at the infamous Cape Cod Coliseum—from the Outlaws, Ozzy, and Charlie Daniels—would create tales to be told back in the hallways at Marian High School in Framingham. Tales like the time during a Charlie Daniels Band show, when my good friend Dave Poisson and I got into a bit of a scrap. We were holding our own against three or four other drunken dudes, albeit with a cracked nose, when a pair of giants, the Ringo brothers, who were working security for the summer, pulled Dave and me from the fray and booted the other guys to the parking lot. Those guys never should have grabbed Dave's cowboy hat. Cowboy up!

As it is with all high school legends, they fade, just as the coliseum faded into memory. Diplomas in hand, friends went off on their own journeys, some to be lost forever. But not the Cape. Stuck in the suburbs, I would pick up a paint brush in the year following graduation, putting money in my pocket while I decided what to do with my life. Of course, I was still wetting a line in nearby fishing holes after painting the latest house on the list. Big Largemouth and Smallmouth Bass would hit the grassy banks regularly, and I fancied myself quite the bassmaster.

I was eighteen in the spring of 1984 when my friend Mike asked me and John Rice to go surfcasting in Mashpee the following weekend. Mike's brother-in-law, Mark, invited us to his mother's house in the Popponesset Beach (poppy) area to fish the surf for early spring Bluefish! It sounded cool to us, but we didn't know what we were in for. Original googans, as it were, with eight foot flipping sticks more suited for a backwoods swamp. But we were new to the surf, and anxious to see what the ocean had in store for us. My "bassmaster" status was officially shelved the following week.

Generally speaking, the southside of the Cape refers to an area of coastline along Nantucket Sound. A beautiful, sandy stretch, some mere miles from Martha's Vineyard, and within eyeshot of the beaches interspersed with inlets and jetties, mansions and beach shacks, incorporating Falmouth to the west to Hyannis in the east. You can throw in the stretch from Hyannis east to Harwich if you like, but the fast action is truly superior along the former stretch. However, I had yet to learn of this on our first visit.

We were true newbies, noobs, and were playing the role of patient students as Mark revealed his surf outfit. These were no freshwater bass rods. No, these were nine to ten foot heavy sticks, loaded with twenty-pound monofilament (these were the days before braided line would revolutionize the industry). At the end of the mono was a heavy barrel swivel, which was tied a leader of forty-pound mono to thirty-six inches. The terminal tackle was complete with a snap swivel, which would soon hold captive the plugs we would be tossing into the light surf at poppy beach. On the southside, the name of the game was topwater action. And in those days, it was about loading the surf bag with the basics: Atom Striper-Swipers, Creek Chub poppers, and the always reliable Robert's Rangers skipping lures. Most of the time, all I really reached for was a two-ounce blue & white Atom, or a 2.25 oz orange Ranger. Honestly, in the mid-80s, these two lures did the trick ninety-nine percent of the time, be it blues or bass.

Prior to the moratorium on the taking of herring & alewives, most northeast anglers, when asked about their top choice for bait in the spring, would fall into two categories: those who fished herring, and those who fished squid. While they both fall into the "striper candy" category, each had its place along the striper coast, depending on location and time of year. Regardless of which camp you ascribe to, the one constant of the spring migration was the unbelievable topwater action that accompanies this time of year. Action so fast and furious that bait buckets were left in the truck bed, and live-wells were left vacant. While there will always be the old salts who simply cannot resist the draw of bait, or the lazy cows looking for an easy meal, for those who have experienced topwater frenzies, and frothing blitzes, there can be no substitute for a well-presented popper, spook, or other topwater offering. And springtime on the south-side of Cape Cod is the place to be.

"Don't wait for the squid boats to show in Nantucket Sound."

When I hear rumblings in the tackle shops in late April or early May, questioning when the squid boats will show, or why they haven't been visible in the sound, that is the first thing that comes to mind. Yes, boats working offshore are a good indicator of bait being plentiful, but the lack of these boats is not necessarily a good indicator of the fishing. Some anxious surfcasters spend their mornings or afternoons patrolling the beach parking lots and coastal causeways with eyes seaward, on the lookout for squid trollers, unaware that rolling in the surf just a few yards from where their tires touch the asphalt, hungry stripers and Bluefish have already arrived. But it wasn't always this way, at least for a good majority of the weekend wanna-be salty superstars.

When I was first introduced to this area as a kid in the early 80's, striper stocks were in a state of desperation. So decimated were their numbers that many states imposed temporary moratoriums along the striper coast. Strict regulations were put in place in Massachusetts, including a one fish at thirty-six inch limit. Hitting this limit was not exactly an easy accomplishment, and most fishermen turned their sights towards Bluefish, with catching a striper being a bonus. But I didn't know this at the time, being somewhat green to the surf-casting scene.

Even if I had been informed, I wouldn't have believed it. Why, you may ask? Because almost every cast during the peak tides would result in either a hook-up, or at the very least, a swirl behind my plug. Big, hungry fish, too busy gorging themselves on squid to realize that the blue and white baitfish or the orange squid they were so hotly pursuing was actually a man-made representation with a deceiving pointy end. Heaving stripers, and hulking Bluefish, regurgitating squid while rolling in the surf.

You always remember your first one! We all know the old saying, but get your head out of the chum bucket... We're talking large, as in large fish, fish that could eat the prizes that my freshwater haunts had rewarded me with over my younger years. My very first surfcasting trip to that previously mentioned southside location resulted in epic topwater action, with blues in the ten pound range and stripers in the mid thirty inch range, capped off with a beautiful thirty-seven inch lineside at dusk. A true jumbo in the lean days prior to the recovery of the bass stocks. My first real surfcasting trip, with many to follow. Some with similar results, some with quite a bit less. As the weeks turned into months, and the months turned into years, my experience grew where I would learn to work the tides, the wind, and other seasonal aspects of surfcasting.

In recent years, particularly since the mid to late 1990's, Striped Bass stocks have rebounded to where their numbers now attract an amazing amount of interest from new anglers, some, no doubt, introduced to the sport by those who pursued their quarry through the golden days of yesteryear, then the lean years, and into the new age of the striper rebirth—fathers (and mothers…can't forget the ladies of the sea), uncles, brothers, and friends, who at one point in time took it upon themselves to take a kid fishing, tying on their first white and blue Atom popper, planting the seed for future generations to carry on our angling tradition. (As a side note - since I first picked up the pen to put these tales to paper a few years ago, we unfortunately appear to be hitting a new crisis on the striper front, one being contested for regulations as the stocks are taking a beating).

Though some years the cyclical nature of bass and blues may lean towards one species having a more dominant presence over the other, the rebound of the Striped Bass fishery was no doubt the biggest influence in the influx of new anglers. But those early years provided me with a foundation built on the shimmering flanks and razor-sharp teeth of Bluefish. The beaches, back bays, jetties, and inlets that line the south cape coast are places where these seeds took root—places like South Cape Beach in Mashpee, and the adjoining Waquoit Bay watershed, or the numerous inlets complete with dueling jetties, stretching from Falmouth to Cotuit. For me and my fishing buddies, the month of May meant one thing... Bluefish were on their way!

Chapter 6

Yellow-eyed Devils of Nantucket Sound

Rodney Dangerfield forever etched into the minds of America the famous phrase "I tell ya', I get no respect." In good old Rodney's case, that comedic declaration was his key to success, and the respect followed. What exactly, does Rodney have to do with fishing? Well, nothing, but that "no respect" factors into the unfortunate mindset of numerous fishermen when it comes to one the gamest fishes that frequents our waters. A fish that can turn a disastrous trip around, a fish that melts drags, shreds line, binds reels, and leaves the heartiest of anglers reaching for the Ben-Gay after waging a day-long battle against wave after wave of razor-teeth and forked tails.

This is the *Bluefish*.

I'm guessing most of us share a common bond when it comes to our introduction into the salty fraternity of the sand and surf. The sharpies of your new-found fraternity plant visions of striped monsters within the comfy confines of your anxious mind, with hardly a mention of the blue and silver denizens of the deep, ravenous choppers that rip up the shoreline, leaving remnants of squid, pogies, or whatever else is unfortunate enough to be sharing the waters.

The Striped Bass gets the accolades, the star treatment, and rightly so. Bass achieve far greater size and present a formidable challenge;

but the yellow-eyed devil is a mighty warrior, committing on every attack in a battle that tests an angler's gear and fortitude. For those of us lucky enough to have encountered gator Bluefish blitzing the surf, there was surely a run on ibuprofen and mentholated balm at the end of the day. Still, Bluefish are treated by some as second-class citizens in Neptune's world, from the online forums where stories of big bass from Maine to Rhode Island consistently stole the limelight, to the tales spun on the rubble-strewn shores of the canal. I'm not saying we run out and start the "Bluefish Master's Classic," but it's high time we show Mr. Choppers some love.

Most surfcasters will tell you Bluefish are easy to catch. "Just throw anything on…they'll hit it!" At times, that statement is true. In the 80's, when stripers were the minority by far, the choppers clearly outnumbered the bass, and some days, every cast had a follow or a strike. So much so, that our crew of guys, girls, aliens, and outlaws would plan the day around it. The whole day! Of course, high tide was the focus, but we'd schedule it out, getting there hours before. Coolers overflowing with beer and ice. Hibachis sometimes. And we'd all catch, using the old standby lures repeated over and over.

But even in those yellow-eyed glory days, certain conditions, lures, and techniques would boost your chances from a good day to a great day. On those less than favorable days, this proved to be even more so. "Southwest is best." That's the response most anglers will follow up with when asked about the ideal conditions for success during the spring. I used to be a firm believer in that statement, but over the years, I've learned to interpret it a bit differently.

Yes, the conditions may be better-suited for both the fisherman and the fish, with warm south-westerlies warming the ocean's surface temperature and keeping the angler comfortable with a hint of summertime in the air. But one thing I've realized is not to let yourself be fooled into thinking you can't catch fish under less-than-desirable conditions. In the springtime, the fish will be there. You may just have to change your approach to finding and catching them.

The coastline along Nantucket Sound offers enough structure and diversity to provide opportunities for those interested in braving less than ideal conditions. Places like protected coves, and the upper reaches of back bays and creeks, can yield surprising results when tossing a small popper and working it along the banks. One of my usual springtime haunts features grass banks alongside sandy flats. When the tide turns and the water starts to rush along the edge of the banks, the bait gets funneled along the edge before dumping into a deep cove, then pouring out into the sound. A perfect set-up for ambushing confused bait. Here, wind isn't as much a factor as tide. On more than a few occasions, I've witnessed feeding frenzies that would turn the aforementioned cove into a boiling cauldron of baitfish, blues, and stripers, in weather ranging from sunny skies, to sideways rain. Regardless of the conditions, tossing a popper into the melee would result in instantaneous hook-ups.

But what to use, you ask?

No matter what the conditions may be, come springtime, as a surfcaster, you will want to have your surf bag fully stocked with a variety of topwater plugs. Conditions and location will dictate what plugs you'll want to reach for first, and experimenting with your technique(s) will put more fish on the beach. For example, in the surf of the open ocean, you may start with an old standby, such as an Atom popper, where you will need to "pop" it at a more rapid pace to keep the action on the top, throwing enough spray to entice the predators from below. However, if the swells aren't too bad, a floating popper such as a Smack-it will allow you to slow down your pop, pausing between snaps of the rod. This can drive blues and stripers berserk until they can't resist taking a slash at the bait.

When the surf is up, but you want to work it a bit slower, you will want wood, and fishing a pencil-popper is a good choice. Under these circumstances, I'll tie on a Guppy or BigFish pencil popper, fishing them in the "walking the dog" style, but in a more erratic manner. If the Bluefish are in heavy, I'll keep Ballistic Missile plugs or Rangers at hand, ripping them across the surface. I've also had big stripers blow up on these skipping lures while in the middle of a Bluefish blitz, so don't hesitate if there is a mix of blues and bass.

In quieter water, such as in the coves and back bays, break out the spooks. Fishing a Doc's spook in the traditional walk-the-dog will have fish pushing bait out of the way to get to your plug. If you're looking for a smaller profile, a Zara Spook should get the job done. Some of my favorite color choices are yellow, pearl white, wonderbread, and copper or burnt orange. I'm primarily looking to imitate a squid, and if I had to pick one color, it's white This holds true for almost all my outings, be it Striped Bass or Bluefish. The key here is to experiment with color, speed, retrieve pattern. There is no wrong choice, but there may be a better choice. The fun is finding out what works.

When I was first (literally) getting my feet wet, I was just a hyped up man-child who worked hard, partied hard, and wanted to learn how to fish hard. But a lot of what I learned about that last one was through experimenting on my own, or was taught to me by old salts toiling away in tackle shops scattered across New England. My friends *liked* to go fishing; I *loved* to fish. There is a difference, and a lot of you reading this will understand.

And so, when the time was upon me to purchase my first rod and reel outfit, I took the advice of a crusty tackle shop owner in a little hole in the wall shop in Cotuit, Massachusetts, on Cape Cod. A place long gone, as are so many others. I needed an outfit right for catching these 1980's Popponesset Beach Bluefish. After shooting the proverbial shit for a bit, I walked out with an eight foot Daiwa surf rod, matched with a Daiwa Black Gold reel, filled with twenty-pound Ande mono. A pretty typical setup for those days, although a bit short compared to the common outfits used today.

If by chance, you spy me at the Raw Bar choking back a cherry bomb, or maybe we cross paths on the sand, and you ask, "what type of surfcasting setup should I get," the easy answer is that it's entirely a matter of personal choice. However, there are some factors to consider. If you're plugging the ocean front, whether it be from the beach or jetty, long distance may be the ticket to reach your target. For example, you don't want to be stuck standing chest deep in water trying to get those extra few feet to reach a school of blues breaking just outside the limit of an eight-foot surf rod, when a ten-footer would've made up the difference from the surf-line.

The opposite is true when working the back bays and short water inside the coves and salt ponds, where that same ten-foot rod would be cumbersome and heavy where a lighter touch is needed. When plugging on the beach, I'll generally stick with a graphite nine-foot surf rod, hoping for the best of both worlds, capped off with a quality spinning reel. However, I do keep an extra ten-foot rod stowed in the truck just in case conditions warrant heavy artillery. For line, it's been a few years, but the move away from twenty-pound monofilament is a fading memory. I now only employ mono in the rare occasion I'm bait-fishing, or trolling offshore. There is a place for mono, but the pros and advancements in braided line technology make it the undeniable winner for strength, diameter, distance, and of course, sensitivity, since there is essentially no stretch.

Finally, I'll top off my set-up with a stretch of forty-pound fluorocarbon leader. Yes, there is a slight risk when it comes to the toothy blues, but for the most part, due to their knack for attacking plugs from the rear, the cut-offs are few and far between.

Now that you've got your set-up, you're ready for your geography lesson.

If Bluefish are your quarry, certain shore locations will produce better than others at particular times of the year, and while I'm not looking to burn anyone's favorite spots, I can at least point you in the right direction by season. For example, it's widely known that the southside of the Cape is the premier springtime spot for blues. A simple glance at a map detailing the stretch of coast from Falmouth to Hyannis will tell you all you need to know when it comes to setting out on your quest.

Incidentally, autumn will see some of these same locations invaded by big choppers on their way south. Plan on two hours before high tide, thru slack, and an hour into the ebb. Also from mid-October to early November, areas at the *end of the world* in Provincetown can see gigantic blues strapping on the feedbag as they prepare for their southerly migration. Concentrate on locations around the harbor and to Race Point for a shot at some of late season jumbos. Summertime proves a bit more challenging, as the water warms up and the bigger fish seek cooler waters. Small to medium-sized blues can still be taken throughout the warm weather as they take up residence in their spring locations, but this is the time when alligator Bluefish will be churning up the rips offshore. There are also options along the shore, places like the outer beaches of Cape Cod or the rocky points of Cape Ann, where cooler water will have some hefty choppers.

South Cape beach is known throughout the region as being primarily a springtime Bluefish hotspot. On any given day from May through early June you can find the beach parking lot lined with campers, cars, and salty pick-ups, rods hanging off the sides, with orange Rangers dangling at the end of half of them. Sure, the bait guys will be scoring with squid and pogie chunks, but this is topwater territory, where ravenous Bluefish are almost always willing to cooperate. I fondly recall one particular day when a school of squid invaded the sound, only to become trapped along the beach where the Waquoit jetty cuts seaward from the South Cape sand.

Big bluefish invade the Cape Cod flats in late Spring

I've been fortunate many times over the years when an unexpected turn-of-events has transformed "just another day" into one for the logbooks, an experience to remember, spawned out of low expectations where an unlikely contributor made all the difference. One of these outings occurred on a cold, rainy, spring day a few years back, when the late April daffodils had us thinking about schoolie bass, prompting a trip to one of our usual haunts on the south-side of the Cape.

When we pulled into the deserted lot, we were faced with howling winds and stinging rain. On this particular day, South Cape Beach in

Mashpee was a boiling cauldron of wet, wind, and sand, and had us re-evaluating our outing. The bartenders and Rum Punch at the famous New Seabury Raw Bar were sounding better and better as the rain pounded at the roof of my truck, but I had one last plan tucked away in my salt-swamped brain. Loop Beach in Cotuit faces east and slightly southeast, just seaward of the cut where Cotuit Bay dumps into the sound. It was a perfect spot to roll the dice, so after the quick jaunt over from Mashpee, we made our way down Main Street and cut over to Loop Beach, pulling into the empty parking lot.

Loop Beach had a perfectly situated parking lot where one could park, hop out, and begin fishing immediately along a stretch of beach just outside an inlet. In those horrendous conditions, with a howling east-northeast wind driving the rain into the east-facing beach, the location offered us a chance at prospecting for fish with hardly any water-logged trekking in the sand, which made sense for our sanity. Conditions were challenging, but we had to at least attempt a few casts. Sitting in the car listening to the Red Sox wasn't going to get it done, so out came the waders, on went the hoods, and with nothing more than a handful of plugs and our surf rods, we cut through the biting wind and cast seaward.

Our poppers were only making it a few yards from the surf-line, and after the first cast we were already to call it quits while laughing at our foolish efforts, when on the second cast, my buddy John was tight to a good fish. The laughing continued, now brought on by disbelief, but then I was "on," drag singing in the rain. Yet it wasn't the Striped Bass we suspected. A school of early blues had corralled squid, pushed up against the beach by the gale, and were anxiously pouncing on our offerings. When we had finally been beaten down enough by the weather, more than two dozen big, racer blues, between eight to twelve pounds, had been released after waging war in a Spring nor'easter.

A different kind of example, where there were no expectations whatsoever, but similar results, nonetheless, took place in a far more welcoming environment, where the freezing, wet conditions were replaced by sun-bleached dunes, and the crashing surf of the outer beaches. The heat radiated off the parking lot as the family and I unloaded the car, grabbed the cooler and towels, beach bags and boogie boards, and set up on a toasty parcel of sand in Truro. A typical summer day on Cape Cod. I hadn't given fishing much thought that day, looking forward to just relaxing and baking in the sun, but I did have one of my older rods and a small plug bag stowed in the trunk. Most of the time, it just gets stuck in the sand, next to our towels, and then gets tossed back in the trunk without touching the saltwater, considering the high-overhead sun. But on that day, it did touch the salt…over and over again, when I saw the boiling water down the beach. I watched as the school moved fast, just outside the sandbar, which now had a few bodysurfers and boogie-boarders riding the waves. Grabbing my rod in mid-flight, tossing on a beat up old Atom popper, and slicing thru the knee-high chop, I secured a place on the edge of the bar and intercepted the blitzing fish, landing five decent Bluefish before they moved out of reach. A few action-packed moments surrounded by summertime and suntan lotion, thanks to hungry Bluefish, and a "what-if" fishing rod. And then there are those times when Bluefish are in the crosshairs, when the surf bag is loaded for war, and the sleek, blue-mirrored choppers are the intended target.

The steam from my smoldering cup of coffee swirled and twisted in the late morning breeze, defying the calendar on this late spring day, as my buddy John Rice and I looked seaward from the parking lot. Although it was mid – May, the temperature made it feel more like April fool's day; but we couldn't be bothered with that. We knew the water temperature was rising with every passing day, and the bent rods at the surf-line told us the Bluefish were in, with determined anglers sporadically battling eight to ten pound choppers. We watched the action from the confines of the cab of my truck for a while. Although the bite was decent, John and I knew that with high tide still more than two hours off, the best was yet to come. Looking to distance ourselves from the crowd, and knowing what the Waquoit inlet area can offer, we decided to make the long trek, approximately a mile and a half west of the main parking lot, and forgo the soft sand of the main beach for the more hardened footpath hidden in the dunes. An easy choice, considering the path cuts through the beach grass, with fragments of an old access road providing a bit more solid of a walk just under the sand. With beach plums lining the way and the marshes to one side, with Nantucket Sound surf crashing on the other, it's a picturesque walk no matter what time of year. In the fall, the dunes come alive with color, but this was spring, and we were interested in what awaited us at the end of the line.

My first forty-pound Striper off the Cape's outer beaches

Chapter 7

Bass Time

By this point, you have probably all figured out that I have a serious case of the blues, one built on salt, suds, and razor-sharp teeth. But seriously, the Bluefish has, more often than not, represented my annual kick-off to the saltwater season. Hunting these fish early in the season can also reveal some surprises, and that is what makes spring so exciting, a time when a Bluefish pursuit can turn into something unexpected. One occasion left a memory of Poppy Beach I'll never forget.

Upon reaching our destination, we stopped short of the jetty by fifty yards and began patiently plugging the surface. My smack-it popper was making quite a commotion in the rolling surf, while John was skipping a Ballistic Missile plug. After only a couple of swirls, we were starting to think that we made the walk for nothing. With still an hour to go with the rising tide, we made the call to stick it out and wait for the tide to slack and see what the turn would bring. But we wouldn't have to wait that long.

The clouds of uncertainty were quickly scattered as my popper was engulfed in a foamy assault, and I was tight to a decent fish. My initial thought was Bluefish, based on recent activity, along with the action we witnessed earlier down the beach. However, there was none of the tell-tale head shaking and scorching parallel runs that typically define a nice Bluefish. No, this fish was running straight out, at a steady and powerful pace, and after a few minutes, a glistening, squid-gorged striper was at my feet.

This was not your normal spring striper. Of course, all the fish are going to be hungry, but more often than not, we'll be catching racers—thin fish, some long and large, others not so large, but still thin. This fish was fat; and I don't mean fat as in your typical summer fish. I mean a round, bloated fish, with squid falling out of its mouth. On most spring days, I'd guess that a thirty-four-inch fish would be in the low teens, but this fish was easily five pounds heavier than what you'd expect. And we were just getting started.

For the next hour, through slack, and for more than an hour into the ebb, we had scores of bass from thirty to thirty-six inches blowing up our topwater baits, each one as rotund as the first. When the action finally died down, the beach was littered with regurgitated squid. We had happened upon one of those rare occasions when a school of predators finds itself in the position to trap a school of baitfish in a perfect location. This time, it was the L-shaped corner where the beach ran into the outgoing jetty wall. With squid as the trapped bait, our topwater lures where the perfect imitation. Poppers, plastic skippers (Rangers and Ballistic Missiles), spooks, each one producing under blitz-like conditions. At one point, the action was so fast and furious that I tied a red-gill teaser in front of my topwater for an instantaneous double hook-up. However, the teaser experiment didn't last long, because mixed in with the fat stripers were the occasional

Bluefish. It was epic fishing at its finest. As the bite slowly died off with the ebbing tide, John and I made our way back towards the parking lot, anticipating the frosty beverages awaiting us in the cooler, laughing at our good fortune and our decision to take the long walk.

The first time I fished Chatham Light, I arrived at my destination as a wild-eyed kid, bursting with confidence that with every next cast, I was due for that elusive, jumbo Striped Bass, a cow of astronomic proportions. And why not? Having put a few good years of surfcasting under my belt, as well as a few good bass, I had recently discovered fishing with live eels—a technique that had resulted in a fair majority of those big bass.

With the sun sinking low, throwing brilliant shadows across Chatham Light Beach, I geared up and made my way down the well-traveled, yet surprisingly rugged and weather-resistant, set of stairs. At the base, I scanned the beach, aglow in the multi-colored hues of the fading light, and headed south towards the corner of a large bowl, where the current ran swift and deep just a few feet from the water's edge. I readied my tackle and began to ply the depths in search of monsters. Well, historic Chatham inlet did not give up one its legendary giant bass that night, but I did catch a few respectable fish.

Why, you may be asking yourself, is the author relaying tales of eel-fishing when this is supposed to be a section concerning drifting swimming plugs? The answer is quite simple. Because of my success that night, I returned to Chatham Light to fish the inlet, and it was on one of those follow-up trips where I was first introduced to the art of drifting the plug.

My buddy John and I had been fishing for a couple of hours. Even with the slithering temptation of a lively black eel, we were having limited success, so I made the call to pack it in and head to the local watering hole for a refreshing beverage. A cold one at the Chatham Squire sounded pretty good after a mostly fruitless night of casting, and not catching. We gathered our belongings and started on the long trek back from the point where the beach previously curved south toward Chatham's South Beach. I say previously, because as most locals know, Chatham and its beaches—particularly around the inlet to Pleasant Bay at well-known Chatham Light—are in a state of constant evolution, with winter storms changing the coastline from year to year. The most dramatic in ages had occurred the previous year, when a new cut was carved out in a storm on North Beach.

As we reached the halfway point, with our footsteps in the sand behind us, a lone figure became increasingly more visible with each pass of the lighthouse's beam. The old-timer's outline against the black current of the inlet gave away the fact that he was tight to a decent fish, and a few yards seaward from his position, his quarry was putting up a decent fight. With a renewed sense of determination, John and I waded out a bit, and proceeded to cast our eels into the current. Minutes passed, and even as the bass were slurping and splashing all about, they wouldn't touch our bait. However, the stranger to our left was releasing another nice bass.

67

That was all I could take. After reeling in, I approached this magician of the sea and asked him what he was doing that was so different from our approach. With yet another big bass in tow, he made his way to the surf-line to work his hooks free. With a broad smile, he clicked his flashlight on. "I'm drifting the plug," he said. There, in the illuminating glow, was a large, pearl-colored Bomber minnow plug, hanging from the maw of a forty-inch striper. A plug that I had fished on and off for years, with limited success, and which usually spent more time in the plug bag than out of it. Of course, that night, we were not loaded up with plugs, but what I learned that night proved instrumental to honing my craft. I learned *how* to fish the plug.

Most fishermen (and fisherwomen) eventually make the transition from bait to plugs as they evolve in their quest to become a better angler. Some will remain true to bait fishing, but for the others, a Finnish-style minnow plug will, sooner or later, find a spot in the tackle box. Some of these original plugs, such as Rapala (which were first hand-carved in Finland), and Rebel lures, were the plug of choice for many of the great fishermen from the golden days of striper fishing. These were the days when such legendary Cape Cod spots like Race Point were giving up enormous bass, a good majority falling to these revolutionary lures. The slim, sandeel-like profile, widely referred to as *Finnish-style*, was a natural artificial in the sandeel rich waters of the Cape. However, out of the box, most fishermen stuck with just a handful of methods when fishing these plugs. Cast and retrieve, or cast, and fish like a jerk bait, snapping the lure, and stopping periodically. And why not? These techniques can have fantastic results, and have accounted for numerous trophies over the years. But certain locations may be more suited for one type of fishing over another, where geographical conditions dictate success by how you work, or perhaps not *work*, your plug. Inlets are such places, and Chatham inlet in particular.

Drifting the plug sounds like a nice, lazy attempt at fishing, when in reality it is anything but that. It requires concentration and an understanding of where your line is at all times. You've got to feel your lure dancing. In locations where the current runs swift, and preferably where there is some form of course-altering structure, bass will hold up and lie in wait for baitfish to come tumbling out of the harbor, pond, or bay.

In certain areas, and with careful footing, you will want to cast slightly up-current, maintaining contact with the lure by slowly, and I mean slowly, reeling. This allows the lure to gently drift, and drum on the surface. When your lure has completed its drift, it will be almost parallel to the shore, and many yards down-current from your position.

Of course, this requires an understanding between the anglers working a particular stretch of water, where you will need to be coordinated in your drifts, so as to avoid crossing lines. This technique is especially deadly at night, where hungry bass will literally be assaulting the plug as it drums overhead, with smaller fish batting the lure with their tails, and bigger fish engulfing it in one vicious strike. You may not result in a fish on every drift, even if the fish are actively feeding, but your lure is sure to draw attention, with popping fishing slapping at your plug three or four times, or even more. Under the cover of darkness, the adrenaline rush is incredible, when the next fish that takes a swipe at your lure, now adrift in these storied waters, may be one of legendary proportions.

In recent years, well-known, local fisherman Matt Zajac, John Rice, myself, and a few select sharpies have carried on this tradition, with phenomenal results. On more than one occasion, we have released fish that some surfcasters don't get a shot at all season.

On one such night, Matt and I were plugging the deeper water to the left of the Chatham Light staircase. With a few hours to go, wading was still not a safe option. As we loaded up our rods and surveyed the water, it was clear that the fish were there, but just out of range, where the edge drops off as the current turns toward the spit of the newly formed sand bar to our right. With the water dropping, we were able to wade out just a bit more. As we moved through the water, baitfish were raining all about, bouncing off the side of our waders, and scattering

Distancing ourselves from each other to accommodate the drifting plugs, we were both immediately hooked up to decent fish, and under the pitch blackness of a new moon, black-colored Mambo Minnows, and Bomber plugs were our weapons of choice. The nighttime blitz continued for a couple more hours until the tide began to slack, and we called it a night. With two exceptional fish of forty-two and forty-four inches in tow, we made our way past the resident skunks that prowl the beach in the darkness, and trudged our way up the stairs, awash in another successful trip in our wake.

. Not every night at Chatham inlet results in a spectacular trip for the logbook, but with careful planning regarding conditions, tides, and equipment, your odds will increase dramatically. Preparation is the number one thing you can do to increase your odds if you are serious about fishing, and being prepared to fish an inlet starts with safety. Any inlet you may frequent will have currents of varying speeds, drop-offs, and channels that may not be immediately visible or noticeable, so take some time to learn your location. This includes getting a feel for the bottom. If you lose your footing on a slick rock in the midst of a barreling current, it could cost your life. Also, keep your bearings. Being aware of your surroundings may get you back on dry land, whereas navigating dips and holes in a rising tide could end up with your waders rapidly filling with water. I have known more than one angler who has lost their footing, including myself, and ended up in the drink. Some are fortunate enough to escape with only a scare. Others, however, are not so lucky, so watch your step.

Now that you've become familiar with your surroundings, you'll want to gear up for success. Exactly what you use, as far as rod and reel are concerned, is a matter of preference, but there are a few things to consider. You will not need to be casting to distant bars, where fish are breaking just outside, as you would say in the open surf. But you will still want the ability to cast to the edge of channels without the burden of an over-sized rod, so leave the ten-foot rods at home. My outfit of choice consists of a nine-foot medium or medium heavy action spinning rod, combined with a quality spinning reel capable of holding at least two-to-three-hundred yards of thirty pound braided line. Typically, I'll top it off with a four foot stretch of forty pound Fluorocarbon leader. I like to keep my plug bag relatively light when working an inlet, considering I may be covering some ground as I work the tides.

Inside my bag you will find seven-inch swimming plugs, primarily Bombers and Mambo Minnows, with a few of my favorite color selections being black, black with a white bucktail, chicken scratch, yellow, and pearl or wonderbread. I also keep one two-ounce Danny swimmer when there may be bigger bait available in the inlet. These are primarily my choices when fishing at night on the Cape's outer beaches. However, during daylight, or low light conditions, I'll add a couple of swim shads, and a popper, where conditions dictate.

Lastly, time and tides can have a major impact on your success. You may get into fish on the rising tide, but to consistently improve your catch, a dropping tide gives you the best shot at bringing home that elusive cow bass. As the bait tumbles out of the inlet, bass will be positioned to ambush, as their prey struggles in the current. Certain locations can vary, but I usually plan on catching at least the last two hours of the ebbing tide, until the flow starts to slack. Also, to increase your odds, fish at night, or false dawn. While you may get into some occasional action during the day, the real fish will be on the hunt at night.

One final thing to consider is the moon. During the height of the full moon, or new moon, tides will be at their strongest. Depending on your location this can either improve or hurt your drifting conditions. If your plug is drifting at the speed of light, it will be out of the zone before you know it. However, in areas where the current is generally at a snail's pace, this may help your drift. I generally try to fish these areas somewhere in the middle of the moon phase, or on either side of the new or full moon.

Striped Bass join the Blues on the flats in search of squid

Chapter 8

Oh What a Lucky Man He Was...

I'm a lucky guy. I have to remind myself of that sometimes, when the nor'easterlies are blowing, and the fish develop a severe case of the dreaded lockjaw. For the most part, I've loaded the memory bank over the years with countless stories of stripers, Bluefish, and various offshore species. But some of my most memorable experiences aren't just a result of enormous fish, or tales of the one that got away. No, some are locked away in a timeless place, because of who I was fishing with, or where I was fishing, or how the trip unfolded into an unusual and unexpected masterpiece of circumstances. And then there are the lessons that are taken from such experiences. One such experience I like to refer to as "Scallopfest."

A few years back, while visiting my sister in Truro, I decided to take my nine year old nephew, Jake, in search of hungry stripers. Knowing that the fish had taken up their usual haunts around Provincetown harbor, we decided to launch my sister's ten-foot skiff, which was wasting away on the beach along Commercial Street, and head out towards Long Point. Pushing through the sailboats and avoiding the whale watch vessels, the little fifteen-horsepower Mercury chugged across the bay. Looking forward more to spending a day with my nephew than actually focusing on the fishing, I had casually thrown a couple of surf rods in the boat, along with my surf bag, and had committed myself to at least getting him a schoolie or two.

Long Point is at the very tip of the Cape, curling back into the bay at Provincetown, MA, and it is truly one of the most beautiful spots you could ever choose to spend an afternoon. Deserted but for the black-capped terns, the occasional gull, and every surfcaster's favorite seabird, the piping *@#!% plover, it was also, unfortunately, desert-like in its willingness to give up a few bass or blues on this early summer day. And so, after an hour of fruitless casting and not yet willing to give in to the possibility of getting skunked, I pointed the creaky bow towards the deep water, and pushed off in the direction of the harbor's jagged breakwater, where I had picked up quite a few bass in the past, while kayaking.

Serving as a barrier against the sometimes harsh Atlantic Ocean, Provincetown's breakwater (not to be confused with the jetty stretching from the west end of town over the tidal flats), runs parallel to Commercial Street, offering protection to the town's pier, Macmillan Wharf, and the many fishing, whale watch, and pleasure boats moored in the harbor. A mere stone's throw from the beach at just a few hundred yards, the rocky structure also provides a perfect environment for Striped Bass to wait in ambush, as baitfish dart in and about the outcroppings, struggling with the swirling currents. As Jake and I slowly approached, the little motor pushing us alongside the breakwater, my expectations were renewed, and I set us up with swimming plugs to slowly troll the edge. At least that was the plan, until I saw the activity picking up at the opposite corner of the long jetty. And the scallop boat.

When we coasted into the mix, the water was boiling with stripers of all sizes, and we were in the middle of a feeding frenzy. The scallop boat had recently set the anchors and the crew was busy with the task of shucking their catch, tossing the guts off the side, and essentially ringing the dinner bell. One other fortunate soul was already tight to a nice bass as he danced around the deck of his twenty-one-foot center console. A member of the crew from the trawler waved us over. Carefully, we eased the skiff over, keeping a safe distance from the rolling hull, as the crewman tossed us a big bag of guts. Quickly swapping out our plugs for unweighted 5/0 hooks, I put some water between us and the big boat, and set Jake up with a ball of guts.

Setting the line out into the current, we were hooked up in seconds, even before I got a chance to let out my own rig. Minutes later, our first fish of the day was in the boat. It then became very apparent that we would not be fishing two rods, as I was balancing the little boat, with a nine year old, and an ocean full of hungry fish. For the next hour, Jake and I caught dozens of stripers, ranging from over-anxious schoolies to three-foot beauties. And, there were some real cows in the mix as well, occasionally rolling on top. I can't imagine the sleigh ride we would've gotten, with the skiff already being dragged around by ten to fifteen pound fish. But, nature being what it is, it wasn't long before those inevitable words were spoken, "Uncle Jamie... I have to go to the bathroom." Just like that, the frenzy was over, leaving Jake and I with an incredible experience, one we're sure not to forget.

That was my first encounter with "Scallopfest," but it would not be the last. Although we had come upon the initial frenzy by chance, a bit of dock chat over a couple cold ones revealed that certain boats regularly set the hook during certain times of the year, and if you kept in tune you had a chance of timing it just right. I have been fortunate enough to partake in at least two more scallop frenzies over the last few years, and on these occasions, we came well-prepared. Rather than armed with extra-long surf rods, and an over-loaded surf bag, seven-foot medium action spinning rods are our weapons of choice, loaded with braid to feel even the slightest pickup, and some light egg sinkers, jigs, and long-shanked hooks, to thread the guts on. The methods have remained basically the same, as the fish are generally locked in, and will take simple, unweighted, baits, drifting down through the tumbling slick of shells and guts. However, if you can get a weighted bait down, you may increase the size of your catch. Jigs and pearl-colored swim shads will also take fish, if allowed to flutter back into the stew.

Although you may find scallop boats from Provincetown to Chatham, and various ports to the north or south, there is another version of Scallopfest we've recently discovered. A somewhat more homegrown version, it involves scuba gear, a catch bag, and a shucking knife, and, in my case, a good buddy who also happens to have just gotten into commercial scallop diving. If you know any commercial scallop divers, tag along one day and offer to help shuck the day's catch, saving the guts in a bucket until you have enough to set up a chum line. It won't be long before the bass are surrounding the boat, fighting over every morsel, as you set your baits out. On our last trip, I think we gave it thirty minutes before the water erupted. If you're interested in trying your luck at scallop diving, look up the Division of Marine Fisheries for recreational and commercial licensing information. Nothing is better than pan-roasted striper stuffed with fresh scallops.

Yes, I'm a lucky guy alright. Lucky enough to have a nephew named Jake who wanted to go fishing with his uncle. My new fishing partner today is a cool dude named Jack Golden, my twelve-year-old son. Jack has some catching up to do before he becomes a salty dog, but he's getting there, with many trout, some blues, and even Mahi-Mahi under his belt!

Chapter 9

Race Point

The first time I saw Race Point, I was greeted by a school of finback whales slowly heading west just off the beach on a cool, sunny day in late April. I had just aired down and made the turn onto the sand when the whales came into view. With the smell of salt strong in the air, I followed the whales up the beach as they pushed the herring towards the famed rip, captivated by the magnificence of this place and its surrounding dunes.

I would eventually discover that the breathtaking views of Race Point can only be matched by the incredible fishing opportunities, stories to be told and retold over the years, for here is a place of legends, where the masters of the surf plied the waters for decades before thousand-dollar spinning reels or braided line existed. Magnificent beach buggies, wood panels, soft tires, linen line, giant plugs, and gnarly sea worms. These surf jockeys would haul in giant fish from sand or suds, launching skiffs right off the point into the Atlantic. These days, a new breed of adventurer is taking to the sea just inches above the surface, plying the legendary waters from atop a kayak in search of jumbo Striped Bass and Bluefish, and my introduction to kayak fishing would soon prove to be an adventure for sure.

A few years back—perhaps much more than a few as the ink dries—in the waning days of summer, I decided to join my sister and her family for a get-together out on the sand at Hatches Harbor. Beer, BBQ, sun, sand and the soothing sound of calming waters on the downtide side of the rip. Just a handful of yards south from the actual tip at Race Point, the fishing can be epic, with stripers and Bluefish crushing the sand eels on either side of the Race. However, the golden days of legends had long passed, and at times it seems as though the fish will never move in, gorging themselves in the rips just off the beach, out of a surfcaster's range. Looking along the surf line, the frustrated shore-bound anglers could only watch and wish as the boats offshore were doing a job on the bass. But I had other plans. Baking in the sun atop my Toyota 4-Runner was my sister's new tandem Ocean Kayak sit-on-top model.

This was before the days of super-outfitted fishing kayak specials. No pedal drive here; we were going primitive! Dragging the Kayak from the roof, I grabbed my paddle and a life jacket and proceeded to sort through my surf bag, paying particular attention to going light. Being a relative newcomer to the world of kayak-fishing, I'll admit I was not completely equipped for the task, as was evident by the bungee cord holding my nine-foot surf rod in the plastic boat, and the surf bag tucked between my legs, as I pushed myself offshore. The wind and surf were both non-existent, so launching was a breeze, no pun intended. Although I may have been relatively new to the sport at the time, I had seen my share of foam, crashing down on my head more than once. As it was, I was finding it hard to keep my beer from spilling even in the flat ass calm conditions!

Ideally, I would have preferred to have a couple of rod holders, holding six or seven foot medium action spinning rods, loaded with braid and a light Fluorocarbon leader. Also, storage compartments would have been handy. Rather than fumbling through a bag of assorted lures in an attempt to find a pair of needle nose pliers without losing anything overboard, compartments provide organization, allowing you to focus more on the task at hand – catching fish. Indeed, the new designs hitting the market every other day are specifically designed for saltwater fishing, equipped with rod holders, compartments, foot pedals for trolling, and other salty accessories. Add to that a little custom fine-tuning, equipped with electronics, and you're talking a serious fishing machine. This day? This was more like a dugout canoe.

The waters around Race Point are loaded with bait. Herring, sand eels, and various other baitfish can all be found in the swirling currents. As I paddled my way offshore, a clear line was visible, the edge of a massive school of sandeels, easily fifty yards long. Digging through my surfbag, I carefully attached a six-inch pearl sluggo to a 1.5 oz. jighead, in preparation for the first drift. My plan was to get up-current, casting at an angle down tide to allow my lure to sink, while my kayak caught up with it. A perfect presentation, and within seconds, my sluggo was trailing behind me in the desired zone. A few seconds later, my rod was almost ripped from my grasp, but immediately my line went slack. There was at least one Bluefish down there. Unclipping my now halved sluggo, I attached a five-inch storm wildeye, hoping to at least give me a better shot at sinking the hook.

The whole area was swarming with life. As I was positioning myself for another drift, I happened to glance downward, peering into the green water. That's when I knew I was setting myself up for a Race Point sleigh ride. Beneath my idle kayak, huge stripers were slashing through the bait, scattering the confused sand eels with their broad tails. It was only a matter of minutes before my first hook-up, and that's when the first sleigh ride began. A nice bass was dragging me through the water, battling not only my rod in hand, but also the weight of the loaded kayak. A few moments later, I brought the thirty-five-inch fish alongside. Not one of the giants I spied below, but a respectable fish none-the-less. Considering we had brought the grill to the beach for a cook-out, I decided to tie the fish off and keep it for the fire. I figured one more would do the trick for the whole family, but I was more interested in hooking up with one just a bit bigger. Half-way through my next drift, I was tight to another bass, one considerably larger than my previous catch.

I was in for one heck of a ride, which brings me to one very important tip to pass along. Think safety first, and proceed with caution in these waters. The seas surrounding Race Point, being one of the most famous fishing locales of the striper coast, can become quite crowded during the season. Commercial and recreational fishermen, and whale watch boats, all share these waters, so keep your eyes in tune with your surroundings. Even then, be prepared for the unexpected. And in some cases, expect a yahoo or two who doesn't exactly know what they're doing. This was one of those cases.

What looked to be a twenty-eight-foot Walkaround was headed directly for my position, appearing to have no regard for the fact that the big boat's wake could easily dump me in the drink. And then there was the fish. While I was paddling in one direction, a jumbo bass was pulling in another. However, just as it seemed I was headed for a swim, the skipper eased back on the throttle, and glided just a few feet off my starboard. At this point, I should've been free and clear of a dangerous situation, but I had a new problem to contend with. The boat had drifted over my line, which was still attached to a very determined fish. I was being dragged into the hull of a bouncing boat. It also became clear as to why the cruiser had borne down on me in the first place. The captain was clearly three sheets to the wind, and his two bikini-clad companions could do no more than giggle and sway. I had to do something to resolve this predicament. With that, I pushed the hull away from me, buttoned down my drag, and hauled as steady as I could. The line popped, the fish was gone, but I wasn't breathing water.

Taking a deep breath, I looked towards the beach at Hatches Harbor and could see smoke coming from the grill by our truck. Considering myself lucky—the thought of a cold beer and grilled striper sounded good—I pointed the nose towards the sand and headed in. I guess the lucky horseshoe was still hanging on, as another thirty-five-inch fish couldn't resist the Storm Wildeye. Two nice fish, tragedy narrowly avoided, and a beachside barbecue. For sheer adventure and a pure adrenalin rush, I'll take a Race Point sleigh ride every time, but don't forget that life jacket – you never know when a wannabe fiberglass hero wants to bring his shitshow to the waves. The golden days of summer would soon give way to the colors of autumn. In my view, it's the most beautiful and rewarding time not only on the outer beaches but all of the Cape.

Chapter 10

Must be the Season of the Witch

The Ghouls and Goblins might soon be amongst us, prowling the dunes, and avoiding the ghosts of pirates past, but the treasures of the season are on full display in autumn. We are treated to brightly colored hues of yellow and red, orange cinnamon on the rim of a pumpkin ale, and grey blue seas under puffs of white peppered skies. The shadows grow long, interrupting the purple dunes in the early light. Sooner rather than later we'll all be gathered around the table, and holiday cheer will wash the glory days of summer and autumn away.

Many anglers will already have hung their tackle out to dry, but for me and others who live the salty life, the season doesn't end when the leaves blanket the backyard. For those who seek the salty life, this nightcap to the season yields the treasure we've been hunting. From blitzes in the Province lands early in the fall migration, to hot Thanksgiving action on the Southside, complete with stuffing and gravy! The "Last Call" of the season is bittersweet, as winter is nigh, but now is the time to extend the quest, for trophies await.

Last call might get you one final drink in the Chatham Squire, but if you head east a bit and make your way out over the rolling dunes of Truro, you'll have a good shot at your best bass of the season. The panoramic beaches between Race Point and Wellfleet will see good schools of fish dumping out of Cape Cod Bay as they head to their wintering grounds. Following the bait around the tip of the Cape, these fish can be intercepted at any time, so it can be hit or miss. One minute it may seem as though the sea is completely devoid of life and the next it is erupting with fish, as boiling pods make their way down the shore. But the years have taught me to not sleep on the opportunities that may or not materialize. As a famous Amity Island Skipper once said, "daylight's wastin'!"

As I pulled into the Head of the Meadow parking lot one late October afternoon, I was pleasantly surprised to find just one other truck, clearly part of the salty dawg allegiance, judging by the well-placed advertisements (see: Striper bumper stickers). Gone were the tourists of summer. Even the lunchtime jaunt down Commercial Street in Provincetown revealed barely a hint of the vibrant colors of summer. My (former) wife and daughter were with my sister, undoubtedly ordering popcorn in line at the Wellfleet Cinemas as the sun kissed the horizon, leaving me free with my thoughts and senses, breathing deep the salt air. The usual surfcasting crowd of the early fall, along with the local surfing combine, were also nowhere to be seen. A more perfect time to be on the outer beaches, I will never know. With my surf bag locked and loaded, I trudged through the dunes where big fish dreams await.

At first glance, the sea was relatively calm, a gentle surf breaking, with the holes and points just starting to show on the ebbing tide. With the driver of the other vehicle in the lot nowhere in sight, I made the call to head north about half a mile to a spot where I had had success in the past. The beauty of the beach, and the color of the great dunes in the autumn light captured me in their glow, allowing me to daydream a bit before my fisherman's senses returned to a welcome surprise.

I'm not sure how I initially missed it. Maybe it was the solitude, the hypnotizing serenity of the lonely beach, but whatever the cause, when I returned from the trance-like state, I was essentially standing next to a pile of treasure. An overflowing pile of silver, with more piles scattered down the beach as far as I could see. After two or three hundred yards, I had walked into an area of beach that had not long ago been witness to a massacre of astronomical proportions, as thousands of peanut bunker committed suicide in an attempt to avoid the snapping jaws and gaping mouths of the predators that forced them onto the beach. Silver for hundreds of yards, yet not the slightest swirl. Knowing full well that I had just missed a "Blue Planet" moment, I dug through my surf bag, selected a crystal minnow to try and match the hatch, and began plying the surf. A fruitless hour would pass until I finally caught up with the fish responsible for the slaughter.

I was fan casting one of the points along the silvery stretch, working my plug with boredom slowly creeping in, when I heard it. Very faint at first, but there was no mistaking it. A splash, just to my left on the edge of the point where the bar drops off, followed by another, and then another. The feed was on, and in seconds the water was boiling. The standard retrieve was getting no results, so I started mixing it up, ripping my plug through the water in a frantic motion. That was key, experimenting with my retrieve until I made them hit. As most fishermen have experienced before, I didn't want to be a victim of "too much bait," when the bass simply will not take an artificial, when surrounded by clouds of baitfish. But not this day. For the remainder of the afternoon, I put bass after bass on the beach, beautiful fat fish from thirty-four to forty-two inches, until the sun faded behind the dunes, and darkness flooded the seascape. Not the giant stripers that makes one a surf legend, but they too can be found if conditions and circumstances are in your favor, as I would soon find out.

Working my way back down the beach, wearing a grin of satisfaction, I was greeted by a lone stranger, the owner of the other vehicle, patiently tossing eels in the fading light. I was surprised to see someone at all, much less someone throwing eels, considering that most bait shops have closed for the season and those remaining open are usually out of eels at this time of year (though I do know of a shop or two that carry them until Thanksgiving). Regardless of his bait of choice, he too had been fishing for most of the afternoon, but apparently I had made the right decision in the direction I took. His journey to the south had resulted in no action whatsoever, although he did say that he had a couple of hits within the last half hour in his current spot just over the hill from the parking lot.

Feeling quite pleased with my success, I was spinning tales of the wild action I had just been part of, when he asked me if I would take a couple of steps to the side. One of the pick-ups he recently felt had resulted in a solid hook-up, and I was standing directly on top of his catch. Buried at my feet was a solid forty-seven-inch Striped Bass, looking every bit of forty pounds. If you can find eels, the bass will find them too.

The outer beaches are not the only place you can find fast and furious action on the Outer and Lower Cape regions during Autumn, even seeing occasional mega-blitzes into November. Some of these locations can be found in Provincetown, not far from Commercial Street. Although most sharpies would be thinking Race Point, the locations I am referring to are just as familiar to the summertime tourist crowd as they are to the late-season anglers in-the-know. Consider that the same fish that can be intercepted in pods off the outer beaches have spent the better part of the fall fattening up for their trek south, to their wintering grounds, and these fish have been ravaging bait in the bay and along the beaches. Two of these late October through early November hotspots are the Provincetown jetty and Herring Cove Beach, and if you're lucky enough to hit them during one of the final dinner bells, bring the Icy-Hot, because you'll be going to sleep with sore shoulders that night.

Some years back, the family and I were visiting my sister in Truro during the first week of November. Being a creature of habit, I've gotten into the routine of taking an early morning coffee run, which had become something of an ongoing joke, where I'd take some time to myself, grab the *Boston Herald*. Yes, the *Herald*—that back page sports headline always got me. For those wondering why I was still buying an actual newspaper… I did say "some years back."

This morning was no different, except instead of grabbing my coffee and heading into the office, I made my way down Commercial Street, which was relatively deserted, and hit the local java joint with a hot cup of Joe in mind. After grabbing a cup and the morning paper, I decided to swing into the lot at Herring Cove Beach to relax and read the paper with the salt and the sand. Passing the empty Parking Attendant's booth, I turned into the right-turn lot (this was before the brutal winter storms that finally resulted in the lot being redesigned), and parked facing the ocean with Hatches Harbor to my right.

Hatches Harbor is a decent stroll down the beach and in the summer it serves as a refuge for millions of sand eels, which end up getting washed out and devoured by multitudes of Striped Bass and Bluefish, along with tuna and whales off Race Point. But this morning, Hatches Harbor was just a chilly walk down the beach, even though I had my spinning outfit in the back of the truck. I was content with my coffee, reading about the Patriots' latest victory, and the sight of dozens of Boobies and Gannets bombarding the depths of Herring Cove, and emerging with dinner in the form of juvenile herring, peanut bunker, and whatever other batfish was unlucky enough to be on the plate.

Boobies and Gannets are large seabirds, and they put on quite a display when diving for their breakfast. Folding their wings from high above, they plummet furiously into the sea, resembling a feathered meteor shower. Ah yes, quite content I was. That is, until I saw the small camper with the Jersey plates.

UNTIL THE NEXT TIDE

Standing with boots at the water's edge, the Jersey fisherman was yelling to his two amigos, as he had just hooked up. I had not set out this morning with surfcasting in mind. That is, not until I saw the size of the Bluefish he dragged onto the beach. It was easily twelve pounds. That was enough for me. With the paper tossed aside, I was out the door with my coffee in hand. As I sat on my tailgate putting on my waders, the Jersey three continued to crush the fish, and now a few stripers were in the mix as well. Topwater was clearly the method of choice, and I joined the action.

When the hits slowed a bit, I edged my way down the beach to the left, in the direction of Wood End. In an area that would be filled with eccentric and exotic nude sunworshippers during the summer months, I found the mother lode. School after school of fish were circling the beach between a minor rocky outcropping and a point just past it, barely forming a slight cove. Bass to thirty-eight inches and blues not much smaller were tearing up my plugs. Surf Howdy sliders, Smack-It poppers, if you could keep it on top for a second, it would be gone in one more. The action continued like this for the next two to three hours, and again with the same tide the following morning. Although, I did not try the afternoon or evening bite, with the quantity of fish around, I am sure the fish would've shown up. But after disappearing for a three-hour coffee run, I had used up my family visit quota.

That was my introduction to the late fall bite at Herring Cove, and the following year produced the same results. Although I will add that I believe timing and meteorological conditions play a part in determining your success, or lack of, as I will admit to being prepared for the bite to happen and I was either too late or too early on one occasion or another. Typically, when the Boobies and Gannets are putting on a show, it usually signifies the end is close, but the possibility exists that schools of fish may be nearby. When a fisherman tells you the season is over, he really means he has given up. But the fish? Well, they don't give two shits and a dime what the fisherman says.

Case in point, I was in Perkins Cove, Maine, many years past now, when an encounter made me rethink the old "fat lady singing" adage. For those unfamiliar with the area, there is a pedestrian drawbridge that spans the cove, and on this particular mid-November day, a weekend family getaway found us crossing the drawbridge, peering into the current below. Looking down into the water, I watched as a school of mackerel was tearing up the water and a bass of at least fifty pounds rolled through it. Indeed, sometimes the fat lady ain't singing, she's merely humming the intro.

Returning to Provincetown, Herring Cove and Race Point aren't the only draws for late season action. Located at the end of Commercial Street is a mile and a quarter long breakwater, a jetty cutting across Provincetown Harbor from the west end of town to a desolate stretch of beach harboring Wood End lighthouse. If there is a more photogenic place on the Cape, I have yet to find it. The jetty at low tide, with the sun setting, paints a picture that truly must be seen, because no written words can do it justice. But as a fishing destination, well I had basically written it off as just a tourist spot for taking romantic pictures. That opinion would change after a stop for a beer turned into tequila and fish tales. Fish tales that included rumblings from local fishermen inside the Governor Bradford Pub.

While sampling some fine beverages inside the infamous tavern, I overheard stories of enormous Bluefish, blitzing alongside the jetty on the rising tide. The next day, I drove down to the jetty fully expecting it to be overflowing with anglers and Bluefish, but there was just the occasional weekender out for a nature stroll. It was late morning, with the tide already dropping, an unfortunate spinoff from the previous day turned into night. But the evidence was quite clear. Signs of that morning's fishing could be seen scattered down the jetty, with the telltale, occasional drops of blood marking the success of the jetty ghosts. The next morning, I would not be late, and for the last two hours of the rising tide, a group of us plugged our way through schools of ravenous, ten-to-fifteen-pound Bluefish. Truly epic.

Chapter 11

It's the Holiday Season…Well, Almost

By mid-month, the second half of "last call" basically shifts from the lower Cape to the south side. Although the action may not be quite as exciting as the first half, there are still plenty of options to stretch the season just a bit longer. The majority of the big fish are now on their way south, heading for happy hour in the Outer Banks of North Carolina. However, for those savvy to the migration and holdover patterns, the bays and inlets on the south side of the Cape will still be holding a healthy population of fish. Mostly school-sized stripers (with the occasional big fish making a surprise appearance), these fish can spice up the holiday season, as they are generally desperate for food and will swarm to your offerings. I have had incredible outings, walking the shoreline of two bays in particular. More noted for their outstanding springtime fishing, the Popponesset Bay and Waquoit Bay watersheds can produce surprising results for the holiday season.

Thanksgiving on the Cape essentially caps the Autumn season. Traffic is but a distant memory, as the Cape takes on a secluded peacefulness, while sea breezes try to stave off the ever-encroaching grasp of winter. I awoke one Friday morning with the forecast calling for unusually mild temperatures, and a turkey hangover beginning to wane. The decision to drive over to Popponesset Beach and take a few casts, where the creek dumps into the bay, was pre-determined before I even opened my eyes. And if I was looking for that secluded peacefulness aforementioned, I wouldn't have to look far.

Today I had this beautiful spot to myself. From atop the stairs leading down to the beach, the bluebird sky, dappled with cotton-ball clouds, reflected off the blue green blanket of a gentle surf below. People sometimes ask me about those times I venture out fishing alone, as if I would be bored. My answer is always simple. These are my times when I'm at church, for there can be no heaven that can top that which is revealed through the sea. Church was in session, as I walked the shoreline looking for telltale signs.

Feeling the sun on my face, I could see ripples in the distance. While not expecting much in the way of quality, I had hoped to at least fool a schoolie or two. The bait darting through the shallows was a good indication that there was still some life left in the season, but what occurred on my first cast was completely unexpected. I let the five-inch mambo minnow fly, and as soon as it touched down, dozens of schoolies came crashing at it from the middle of the channel. From there, it was a fish on every cast, including a double-header where both trebles found incredibly determined bass. What started as a peaceful walk on the beach, soaking up the Indian summer rays, ended with a blessing and a waterman's grin. Truly, I had much to give thanks for. But sometimes, you leave the bird in the oven just a little too long, and the holiday plans don't quite play out as you hoped. Such was the case for my old friend Mark, who headed out one late fall day with hopes of giving thanks to the fish gods!

We had been hearing tales of huge Bluefish in mid-November being caught on diving swimming plugs at the Waquoit jetty for a few years running—first-hand accounts that tempted us to forgo the warmth of a fire, cold beer, and football. I hadn't given it much thought for some time when a friend from the days of my surfcasting baptism passed on a recent report. Mark had been able to come across some live eels and had trekked out to the jetty late in the afternoon to work the dropping tide into the night.

The jetty at Waquoit Bay is approximately one-and-a-half miles from South Cape Beach in Mashpee, when walking the path to the right of the main parking lot. A bit of a walk, but the payoff can be worth it. Upon his arrival at the jetty, it was immediately evident that the Bluefish were there, as his eels started coming back after each cast as cigars, so he worked his plugs and caught a couple as the sun set. With the light fading he switched back to eels, and within just a few casts he was tight to a good fish. With the fish on top after about ten minutes, he could see it was in the high thirty-to-forty-pound range, and was showing signs of being just about ready when the sound of a boat entering the inlet came over his shoulder.

With arms waving in the creeping darkness, and shouts to alert the skipper being drowned out by the motor, all he could do was watch as the boat skimmed over his fish and the line went slack. If you have ever lost a giant fish, you know the feeling. If you're a guy reading this, and have never lost a giant fish, the physical equivalent is like taking a knee to the cajónes… It hurts, and takes a while to get over.

UNTIL THE NEXT TIDE

That weekend, we ventured out for a little pre-Thanksgiving celebration, and battled jumbo blues as they chased the remaining bait through the jetty, hitting the diving plugs with the intensity you would expect from hungry choppers.

Chapter 12

Northern Exposure

I suppose it is only coincidence, or possibly a matter of fate, that northern exposure as I know it started in Ogunquit, Maine. The Abenaki Indians named it "beautiful place by the sea." Sometime in the early 70s, my folks were driving south from somewhere Downeast Maine. That is, until they broke down in a little, eccentric town, south of Kennebunkport. Thus began the love affair with one of the most breathtaking stretches of beach in all of New England. Ogunquit lies smack in the middle, between York Beach and Wells, and features one of the worst stop light intersections found on Route One, which, by the way, starts at Mile Marker 0 in Key West, Florida. So the observation about that intersection is really saying something.

But, for as much as that little intersection is a pain in the arse, it is also the gateway to Ogunquit Beach. I happily admit the "exposure" part is partially a pun, given that Ogunquit was a place where the Quebec tourists were happy to let it all hang out, which made those beach walks with Dad extra special. There were not boobies and gannets here. Just boobies, nyuk, nyuk, nyuk (Three Stooges fans rejoice).

It's funny what a young boy's mind retains, like going to the movie house in the little downtown area. Dad, always a James Bond fan, of course took us to see *The Man with the Golden Gun*. When Roger Moore comes upon a stunning Asian beauty swimming naked in a pool, who teasingly introduces herself as "Chew Mee," that left a lasting impression on my brother and me! All joking aside, following that fateful day when the car shit the bed, Ogunquit and the surrounding areas evolved into a summer destination for our family for years to come, an annual getaway for a week or maybe more. In the early days, these getaways might be a cabin rental near Flagg Campground in York Beach, then later to the Betty Doon Hotel in Ogunquit Center, and finally, to a family cottage on the Marginal Way, Ogunquit.

The early years at York Beach were about body surfing, checking out the pretty girls, and stealing kisses by the beach near the Sun and Surf beach shack. When I think of Maine today, I see those early years in my head and I can hear the surf and the music on the boom box, a trip down nostalgia lane of 70s pop…think *Guardians of the Galaxy* soundtrack, and you'll hear it. And how could I forget busting my little toe, sliding down the rock wall along the beach, but being too cool to tell anyone. Of course, there was York's Wild Kingdom, an old school amusement park that still makes me smile.

As a young kid, I hadn't been bitten by the fishing bug yet. If I had, I know where I would've fished. While everyone has a hard time resisting the area surrounding famous Nubble Lighthouse, that location remains for me, to this day, simply a great place for a family picture—astoundingly picturesque, but not a great spot to burn hours casting. If I was a young rock hopper back in those days, I would have spent my time chucking lures over the rocky patches on the southern end of Long Sands beach, where Striped Bass lurk. More recently perhaps twenty years ago now), the same location has produced plenty of bass for me, from shore and boat.

One of the more interesting trips around York was courtesy of an invite from an old friend, Tom Gorham. Tom and his wife Kelly (who also happens to be part of the ol' Framingham crew) live on the York River, where they conveniently moor their boat. Tom's brilliant, red-hulled twenty-four-foot Chris-Craft was a sharp looking vessel to be sure, but its sole purpose this day was to get us into fish, as we went in search of stripers and blues along York Beach.

A quick stop at Anthony's Market on Route One for a couple of prime rib n' egg breakfast sandwiches got the morning off to a good start, and shortly thereafter, we were gliding down the river to the open Atlantic. Long Sands' rocks produced a couple of small bass, as did the ledges on the approach along the shoreline toward Nubble Light, but for the most part it had been a slow outing. The ride back, however, would change that around quickly.

As we made the bend in the river before the Route One bridge, a flurry of activity was apparent. The water had sporadic boils, as big fish had trapped bait just outside the marina. The bite was on small bait, short-lived and tough to work in the current; but we managed to hook a few. The one that stood out was a huge Bluefish, easily in the mid-teens, which destroyed a pink sluggo on a jighead. Typically, I'd be psyched for such a great fish, and I was to a degree, but the fish swimming just under the big chopper was what spiked the anxiety. A massive bass, over forty inches, round and heavy, made a play for the jig that the Bluefish whacked. It quickly lost interest in the halved sluggo, as I frantically tried to get the jig back in the zone. Nevertheless, a great day, one which reminds me I need to reconnect with old friends when the tide rises.

Heading a bit north, the coast remains a ragged, angry expression of granite cliffs and ledges, rumbling cuts with crashing waves, until it runs into the Ogunquit River, where a reprieve awaits and the shore turns to sand for a long stretch through Ogunquit north through Moody Beach and Wells. Ogunquit Beach is a well-known and highly regarded spot for northeast surfers, as is Long Sands in York. But Ogunquit has a more colorful vibe, with a gay-friendly community, and is more laid-back than the funky surf-beat scene of York Beach. Both are amazing spots for vacations, weekend escapes, or even day trips, but for the surfcaster, Ogunquit Beach wins hand down. The variety of natural structure means an angler has numerous opportunities and waters to fish, thanks to Mother Nature; and the same coastal formations that makes this attractive to fishermen also make it a seaside playground.

A couple of decades removed from the disco days of Roger Moore's James Bond, the man with the Golden gun was replaced with a wife, a (step)daughter, and summertime escapes to a family cottage that overlooked the Marginal Way. Of course, there were also weekend getaways, with our daughter Kasey safe and secure at home with family sitters, allowing my ex-wife Gina and I to party with our pirate friends, storming the Ogunquit seaside fueled on rum and rock n' roll. The early 90s were a bit of a blur; but when the fog cleared and the sea called, the golden gun was replaced with a graphite spinning rod, equipped with a teaser in front of a swimming lure, doing its best impersonation of a baitfish chasing a sandeel.

By the end of the decade, there was a little less rum, and a whole new appreciation of the beauty of the fishery Ogunquit had kept hidden from me. The Bloody Marys could wait until Sunday mornings, but before the sun would pry my eyes, the singing of a drag being tested would highlight the tumbling waves.

The orchestra that played on every wave didn't need the accompanying sizzle of a tight spinning reel. Even now, if I close my eyes I can still hear the pebbles being sucked out on every retreating wave, being bottlenecked between the rocky points, jagged instruments with each note. A bit dangerous? Sure, much easier to rock-hop and fish under a blue and white, *Toy Story* sky. Easy to throw lures to the white water off the granite, where schoolies and occasional bigger fish would entertain. Maybe even a few pollock; although they would be more suited being tossed back out on another rod as a live bait for bigger bass. Indeed, hiking along the Marginal Way casting swimmers and soft plastics is a great way to spend a Summer day. But if you're looking for more of an Indiana Jones type of adventure, best gear up for a nighttime commando raid of the Striped Bass lurking near the mouth of the Ogunquit River.

My first memory of fishing the Ogunquit River was actually more of a self-taught lesson in gigging. What's gigging, you say? Well, for a ten-year old kid, it was my way of playing Jacques Cousteau.

Gigging is basically spearfishing with a wooden pole and a pronged spear fashioned to the end. This was my choice when snorkeling the river. Never mind that the water could be in the fifties or even colder some days. That didn't stop me from donning a scuba mask, grabbing a catch bag, and taking the plunge. More often than not, my bag would contain flounder and lobster when the chill finally caught up with me. Decades later, the chill was still there, but it took a lot longer to reach me thru the chest waders as I navigated the sandbars and rocks of the river mouth.

The river doesn't particularly stand out at high tide, more of a swollen and sunken marsh in appearance, wrapping the spit of Ogunquit Beach from the mouth northward towards Wells, Maine. But as the tide ebbs it reveals its beauty, carving the marsh and the back beach to the opening at the seafront. While the incoming tide will carry fish, and can produce great angling opportunities, the dropping tide allows a surfcaster access that is much more difficult, if not impossible, during high water. But this is also dangerous water, with a current that rips at an extreme clip, with deep edges along the bars. During the day, this makes for a great time floating down the river for summertime fun. Fishing can also be good at times during the day, like one July 4th where the stripers were literally swimming through my legs. That day, the corners of the river, where the current really cranks, held thousands of schoolies throughout the tides, and low water would put you right on them. If the tide was right, this can be a fly fishermen's paradise, when you can cast off the bars into six feet of crystal clear water. However, for the adventurous surfcaster, coming back twelve hours later for the night ebbtide puts you in the heart of your own paradise.

As is typical of fishing the surf at night in Maine, other anglers are scarce. More than likely, you'll be alone under a squid-ink sky with the stars and the salt. Such was the case when I ventured out from the family cottage, walking along the Marginal Way toward the beach. Just after the rocky point where the river opens to the Atlantic, I carefully climbed the jagged granite down to the river, where sub surface reveals a sandy bottom with scattered boulders. When I say take care and watch your step, I mean proceed with extreme caution, as both sides of the river here are extremely dangerous, especially at mid-tide, when the current is flying and the drop-offs come in feet not inches.

I heeded my own advice, not wanting to leave my family comfortably asleep in these wee hours only to awake to a search party. But my mission was clear and my mind focused. My nine-foot surf rod and light surf bag were readied prior to touching the water. The business end of my fishing rod had my "go to" at the time, specifically for these conditions – a five-inch olive-colored Yo-Zuri Crystal Minnow with a small, plastic Redgill sandeel teaser about thirty-six inches up the leader attached to a dropper loop. If this sounds complicated, it's really not, but the resident Striped Bass didn't care one way or the other.

My first cast drummed in the current as I slowly retrieved my lure. With an occasional twitch imitating a frantic impulse of baitfish, it was only a matter of seconds before I felt the first strike, as a hungry striper found my teaser. The same results repeated themselves over and over, on almost every cast, as I searched though the school-sized fish holding along the far sandbar, looking for a big mama. Navigating further towards the mouth where the river bottlenecks slightly, I found what I was looking for. The drag on my reel started singing immediately, as the bass made a straight shot toward the open ocean, the current aiding in its attempt to escape.

A break in the rocky shoreline was the perfect spot for the landing, and I slid a beautiful thirty-six-inch fish, which had the Crystal Minnow in the corner of its mouth. The tide continued to drop as I moved closer to the oceanfront until the sky started to turn a greyish shade of pink. I now found myself out front, with frothy waves picking up as the tide turned even as the river continued to drop. The fishing I had already deemed incredible was capped with a blitz out front, with birds crashing and bass of all sizes feeding in the surf.

Shifting gears to the beach is prying a story from the salt-soaked inner-layers of my Davy Jones mind, when a beach day with the family evolved into a night filled with giants. The humidity and temperature defied the calendar, more fitted for July than Labor Day weekend; but it was perfect for kayaking the refreshing flats out front of the beach as the river poured out and over the now shallow sand bars. My daughter Kasey and her mother Gina splashed through the slight waves in nary two feet of water. I pushed the nose of the kayak into the bigger surf just outside the shallows, and over a relatively deep trench where sandeels were schooling. The waves were giving me quite a workout, trying to maintain my balance while also trying my best to actually surf down the front. I'm guessing I ended up about 50/50 in attempts. Not too bad considering I probably looked like King Kong trying to ride a banana peel down Mt. Washington.

Knocking the saltwater from my ears, the tide was beginning to flood a bit more, so I headed closer to shore. Something ahead caught my eye, as I approached the deep trench. The dark cloud of sandeels, thousands, maybe millions, I really don't know, was no longer one cloud. It was fragmented, being scattered, and then regrouping as massive, cohesive unit, an organic machine held together by the magnetic pull of "safety in numbers." But the large shadow splaying out over the flats wasn't fooling the squadron of Striped Bass closing in. Monster-sized fish, not only for Maine waters, but for the haunted striper grounds up and down the coast, blazed thru the cloud, instantly turning a sunshine kayak ride into a desperate paddle to the beach to retrieve my rod and a few lures. I spotted fish I estimated at twenty to forty pounds streaking beneath me as I crossed the trench. It was one of those few moments that is instantly burned into your mind as a salty dog. In what felt like hours, rather than minutes, I had gathered my gear and quickly spun about, hearing only white noise from our towel. Alas, those minutes really did make a difference, as the quickening pace of the flood tide pushed enough water into and over the flats, allowing the baitfish trapped into the trench to escape to deep water. The remaining scales were all that was left as the bass and their prey moved on. Frustrated, but buzzing with adrenaline, I glanced at the time as soon as I was back on the beach, and planned to return in the evening. When the flood would again be approaching the same stage of tide, I'd be ready if the fish returned for a midnight feeding!

Sometime before midnight, I quietly pulled into the Ogunquit Beach parking lot, making sure to dim my headlights before coming to the stop, the beach sprawled out in front of me. The lights from the lot threw just enough illumination to indicate the tide was exposing the vast shallows and trenches, with barely a slight chop, inside of the big breakers that are typical off the beach. With the tide still not quite up to my liking, I decided to grab my gear and the bucket of eels I had procured earlier in the day, and make my way left, down past the Norseman Hotel. Soon, I happened upon a nice bowl with sandy points on each side. The disappearing white water told me that we had relatively deep water in close, where otherwise you had a steady stream of gnarly rollers over the shallower water.

Now, it may not be easy, but I love fishing eels. Big, black, slimy snakes, they can drive an angler nuts, curling into a tangled mess, fouling line—but hot damn, they are striper magnets! The key is keeping them cool, even to the point where I would get a small shoulder cooler with a hard inside shell, and put an old rag and a Ziploc bag with a bit of ice in it. The ice would chill them down, making them less spastic, and the rag gave you a better grip on the slime. Hooked through the lower lip and then through the upper, I cast out into the hole and began an extra slow retrieve with the unweighted snake. Close to shore I felt the unmistakable tap-tap of a fish. Lowering my rod tip, I let the line come tight and set the hook. Not a giant, but a respectable thirty-two-inch fish was soon to be released into the dark Atlantic. By now, the tide was flooding in, and it was time to backtrack to bass trench.

Following the shoreline, and rapidly nearing the river-mouth, I spotted the dim glow of a solitary lantern in the distance. I presumed that glow to be accompanied by at least one other angler. As I closed on my target, it became apparent that there was but one fisherman. To my delight, he had his back to the trench and looked to be fishing chunk baits, probably mackerel. I went into stealth mode when I reached the location of the day's reveal. I couldn't make out anything under the swift currents, and there were no tell-tale signs of feeding on top for the eyes or ears to confirm, but I knew there were giants in the area.

That certainty was soon confirmed as my first cast into the flooding trough was hammered by a massive fish, which hit so hard it was peeling line out of the deep water instantly. Clearly it was in the shallows now, trying for the white water of the open sea, and then… it was gone. Heartbroken and pumping, I prayed this didn't spook the whole school. However, my second cast was engulfed as quickly, and I was off the races, and rounding the bend. This fish took me toward the river somewhat, before I had it swim right up on the sand. The third cast was a repeat of the first two. Two back-to-back twenty-to-twenty-five-pound class fish, and the whole trench to myself.

I was mentally patting myself on the back saying, "you lucky bastard… you got this all figured out," when disaster struck. The dark and mysterious figure on the other side of the sandbar was giving up as the surf was rising, and he was heading toward me, not knowing that there was a school of huge bass between us. The now-deafening sound of the surf masked my yells for him to go the long way around, and then he stepped into the trench. As the wader-clad figure emerged in front of me, I not-so-kindly let him know that he just walked through and spooked a trophy class school of bass. The crusty old fart ignored me and head low, vanished towards the parking lot. Thirty minutes later, without a bite and with the tide getting dangerously high, I packed up my memories and headed for some shuteye.

With the old beach in Ogunquit having gone by the wayside, I've scaled back my expeditions to Maine in recent years. But I still always bring the surf gear with me on our family summer outings to that *beautiful place by the sea*. The bass are still there, but these days the beach is the real star. It really doesn't get any better than floating down the river to the salty flats with family and friends, a cold beer in hand, and lobster awaiting down in Perkins Cove for dinner. But yes, a fishing fool always take a few casts.

The Downeast expeditions may have evolved into "toes in the water, ass in the sand" retreats, but in the last decade plus, a salty new obsession has taken hold. It begins with a slow burn, when the first reports start to trickle in sometime around mid-August. Every day, scanning social media and other various outlets I might use, a new picture emerges, fueling the fire. The hint of fall in the lengthening shadows of the waning days of summer is a prelude to the colors to come of red, yellow. But, before we see this brilliant palette unfold across the autumn landscape, the colors I've waited all year for soon grace our in-shore waters. Silver, blue, and green! The tropics have arrived in New England!

Chapter 13

The Silver Bullet Express – Cape Cod

My obsession with False Albacore didn't really evolve into what us Northeast fishermen call "albie fever" until sometime in the mid-2000s. At that time, the primary season for albies being in autumn was overshadowed by what was a resurgence in the Striped Bass fishery, and most of my surfcasting focus was still on the great outer beaches of Cape Cod. But it wasn't only what the purple-tinted, twilight sands of the Cape's dunes had to offer. There was a tsunami of Boston sports spreading their own fever across the region.

The New England Patriots dynasty was establishing itself as one of the greatest of all time. Brady! Belichick! Lombardi trophies! And then finally, in 2004, after eighty-six years, the Red Sox finally broke the curse of the Bambino! Oh, those Yankees fans loved to rub it in our faces right up until the historic comeback, down 0-3 in the American League Championship Series. Shit, let's face it, they had every right to gloat. History had not been kind to the Sox over the World Series drought. Even the previous year saw the Red Sox collapse against the very same Yankees in seven games. But all those years of frustration soon faded away as Johnny Damon's game seven grand slam put the nail in the "Evil Empire's" coffin. The Sox would go on to win that World Series, and a few more.

The two decades that followed saw the emergence of fair-weather fans like we've never seen in these parts, kids that never knew losing. Eventually, winning was so commonplace, I couldn't blame New Yorkers or other rival cities from being put-off by the arrogance that spilled over the border. By the late 2000s, the shine of the trophies didn't occupy as much time on my schedule as it once had, and the draw of giant stripers, while always thrilling, didn't challenge me as much as it used to. Many big fish had come to the sand or over the rail in the previous two decades, and I needed a new challenge. The weekly reports in September and October always included a few accounts of silver bullets being caught along my typical, springtime Bluefish haunts. I had found my quest – I was going to catch albies from shore!

My actual introduction to False Albacore, aka albies, little tunny, appleknockers, silver bullets, fat albert, bonito (in southern states, particularly Florida), and their scientific name "Euthynnus alletteratus," actually took place quite some time before I took up the quest. I believe it was the late of Summer of 1990 or '91. I was living in Sandwich, Massachusetts, on Cape Cod, taking summer classes at Four C's (Cape Cod Community College), and painting houses to help with the bills for the house my sister and her girlfriend (now wife) Eileen had rented in Forestdale.

The money wasn't great for tradesmen in those days, but I loved painting, being outside, and my boss, Rick Enz—owner of Rick's Painting—was a decent and a fair guy. One day, Rick treated the crew to a day off and a charter on one of his buddy's fishing boats. Ripping and trolling wire line for stripers was common practice in those days, and we set out for Monomoy. The day was filled with numerous large Bluefish, and bass to thirty pounds, with the exception of one unexpected visitor. That day, a green-backed silver fish with tribal markings found a trolled hoochie irresistible. It damn sure looked like a tuna, but a fraction of the size, and the power and speed you'd expect from the fork-tailed big cousins.

You wouldn't expect much from a football-sized fish on wire line, but it made its presence known to all on deck. That was my first exposure. The second would plant the seeds of what would grow into a yearly challenge, fueling the fever as summer turns to fall.

The early 90's saw me and my friends dipping our toes more and more into the blue water scene. Sure, bass trips to the shoals were still common; but now, trips to warm, gulf stream eddies, or channels where behemoths roamed, were interspersed with our other expeditions. One particular trip, maybe around '93, found us hunting Yellowfin and Bluefin Tuna to an area called the Mud Hole off Block Island, Rhode Island. It was nothing less than red-hot action, and taking a second to crack a beer or hit the head would undoubtedly end with at a triple hook-up, if not all rods bending. Naturally, by the time we were back at the dock, we were already planning a return for the next year.

In early October of 1994, John, Gary, and I found ourselves unloading our gear in a cheap hotel somewhere near Narragansett in preparation for an early departure the following day. But first, dinner and a few beers were on deck. To this day, I haven't been able to figure out where it was. Somewhere between 'Gansett and Point Judith was a hole in the wall, with typical pub grub, stuffies, rum, and beer. Of course, we partook in all; but the one memory that hangs in the air like a strange and twisted fog, was the gentleman that occupied a corner booth, accompanied by a pretty blonde.

While the blonde would normally draw the glances from the scurvy dogs abusing the air in this corner of the map, and others uncharted, it was the man who stirred a sideways conversation. By themselves, the plaid shirt and blue jeans was nothing of note; but the picture soon became more colorful when you added the red bandana rolled as a headband, the reddish grey beard, and more notable, the double reddish grey braids, long and framing a wizened face. If this wasn't the "red headed stranger," then God or some other supernatural influence was playing a trick on us. That night, Willie Nelson, or Willie Nelson's doppelganger, was drinking Budweiser in a smoky dive bar, closer to Canada than Texas.

The next morning came early, with red eyes, foggy brains, and the need for coffee, as we checked out of our hotel, singing "On the Road Again." We wrangled up some nasty java along the way, and pulled into the Port of Galilee, eyes peering through the wee hour's darkness for our charter. The cabin was aglow, the yellow beams slicing through the misty black, and the hum of the "Sea Hawk's" diesels played the soundtrack of a working fishing port. The sand was yet to leave our eyes when the wish for a repeat of last year's epic venture was soon broken. The skipper informed us of high seas, which we took him at his word, as we were all familiar with rough weather. We opted to forgo an inshore trip for bass, and settled on rescheduling for the next season. However, the day was young, as they say, and we were loaded up with surf gear in case we wanted to make a few casts around South County. The East Wall jetty at Point Judith was literally right down the road, so what better place to pitch plugs to the sea gods?

The dirt parking lot at Camp Cronin already had a couple of cars seaside, and the jetty sprawling out in front of us had a few bait soakers already trying their luck for scup. Looking left, some whitecaps were breaking the surface of the grey-blue swell, kicked up by the aforementioned high seas offshore. With the sun creasing the sky to the east, Point Judith lighthouse kept a watchful on the rocks below, as adventurous souls rode the swell and braved the seas below in search of fish dreams. Three hungover dudes, we were doing our best to navigate the rocks atop the jetty while we aimed for the first bend.

The jetty is a relatively easy walk, at least the first two thirds, with only one spot where you may need to do a bit of climbing. But that last third? Well, I've done it, and I don't recommend it. Every few feet you're doing a bit of bouldering, up and down, and repeat, only to find the fish either out of reach or disinterested enough to make you ask yourself why you should bother. The smart call is sticking to the unbroken stretch, where we now stood, tying on two-ounce popping plugs with the intent of fooling any Striped Bass or Bluefish looking for bait pushed towards the wall.

It wasn't "lights out" fishing, but pretty damn good, as every few casts, a big Bluefish or schoolie bass found the pointy end, saving a blown-out trip. Then, abruptly, John was tight to a monster. His white Atom popper had been slammed, stripping twenty-pound monofilament line (braid was still relatively unknown) at record speed, with power that must have been coming from a huge bass.

I climbed down the side of the jetty, poised to get my hand inside the maw of a giant striper, when I saw the first hint of color. Something wasn't right here. Where was the fish ripping drag like a rocket? Was it under the shimmering, silver platter before me? Then I recalled the fish from Rick's painting charter from a few years prior. A False Albacore! We were in disbelief even after I wrapped my hand around the tail of what may have been a seven-pound fish on a good day. The seeds took hold that day, and the roots of the quest began to grow.

Surprisingly, the leaves of the quest didn't really sprout for a good baker's dozen years. It wasn't for lack of want, but more a result of my friend Gary's new expedition, which saw him embarking on his own quest, the search for the wreck of a late 18th century sailing vessel, laden with riches. I spent a few years helping out, along with some other buddies, as deckhands when time allowed. Don't be misled; this didn't feel like work. Gary's dream of treasure was alive and well, and still burns to this day. For us fish pirates, however, it was more about being on the water, laughing, drinking beer, listening to the Dead and Bob Marley, and more importantly… tuna fishing. But that's a story for a later chapter. When the quest returned, it came roaring back, and by the latter half of the 2000s, the albies took center stage. My surfcaster's blood tingled with anticipation. I was committed to catching one of these silver bullets from shore.

I'm not sure what year it was, but the autumn days were ticking away as that September turned to October. The fall had been particularly warm that year, and we had a very good showing of large Striped Bass on the southward migration, but by Columbus Day weekend, I was ready.

I've always loved the fall, September and October especially, and not just because my birthday falls almost to the day (Indigenous People's Day now, but my Irish, Italian, French Canadian, and sliver of Native American heritage can't make up its mind). The fishing can be off the charts great! Stripers, Bluefish, Bluefin Tuna! And that holiday weekend, I was determined to add False Albacore to the list. High tide at Popponesset Beach on Cape Cod was bit later in the morning, but from my asshole stepfather's house in Bass River, it was a good thirty-minute drive.

My wife Shannon, my son Jack, and I had come down for the weekend, and my buddy John arrived to join me on the quest. We left shortly after sunrise, wanting to give the flats a bit of time to flood, and soon thereafter, we were pulling into an empty small lot where fishermen's parking was available with an overlook to the beach and jetties below. This spot was well known to us from decades of springtime Bluefish expeditions, and usually has a full lot, so to find it empty prompted a bit of insecurity. After all, I was still a newbie at the shore-caught albie game. But those insecurities would fade in an instant as soon as we stepped onto the overlook. Below us were turquoise seas, under a brightening day, with temps climbing into an unseasonal mid-80s degrees. A true "Indian Summer" day. But the sun made the visibility exceptional, and the clean water below us surrounding the jetty to the right had Sunday morning fishing-show-action playing out before our very eyes.

Clamming the flats with my wife Shannon and baby Jack

The jetty was the main focal point, but that which surrounded the jetty drew one's eyes to the nervous, brownish cloud encompassing the rocky structure. A giant baitball of peanut bunker, specifically known as juvenile Atlantic Menhaden, had the jetty locked up. In an instant, a slashing split of blue, opened and closed through the mass of baitfish as a pod of albies were using the jetty to pin their prey from both sides. Quickly grabbing our boots and gear, we hustled down the wooden steps and haphazardly scurried to the end of the jetty.

The end of my nine-foot surf rod, reel filled with fifteen-pound mono (I would soon join the braided line movement, of which I'd never turned back), and twenty-pound leader, sported an Ava Maria jig, an epoxy-type jig that was the basis for the creation of Mike Hogan's, Hogy Lures epoxy jig. A staple in every albie fisherman's bag today. The "maria" jigs were highly regarded for inshore pelagics, and have been discontinued for a decade. But on this birthday, I had a one-ounce blue/silver jig primed and ready to cast.

As is typical of many irresponsible fishermen these days, seconds before I was set to make my first cast, a twenty-one-foot center console came ripping down the shoreline, coasting right up to just off the jetty. Making matters worse, the selfish prick hooked up immediately. These were my fish. I was not letting this slide. As I gave him an earful, I cast directly toward his boat. The skipper smartly turned his bow in the opposite direction as I cast again. Once, twice, thr… hooked up! My first little tunny from shore!

The fish did everything I expected it to, including spiking my blood pressure and charging me with adrenalin. My mono line sizzled off my reel, and what seemed like one hundred yards vanished from my spool. I fought the fish low, keeping the line tight, but with a soft touch, and made my way to the beach, hoping for a safer landing spot. Minutes later, the first step in my quest was complete, as I slid a beautiful silver, green, and blue albie to the sand. I was in another world, with a birthday present you would wish for. My wish had been granted, and the best birthday now presented itself to me.

John congratulated me, and it was then I heard the sound of added applause from behind us. This is when the adventure gets slightly twisted. There on the beach behind us, were a group of women who could easily have been mistaken for the "Jersey Shore" girls. Apparently, they had come down the stairs from the street above, where they were renting the sweet beach house, setting up for a day of sun and cocktails on this hot, October day. Normally, I'll always release an albie, as they aren't known as good table fare. As a matter of fact, some would say downright awful; but they are a spectacular gamefish. It was when I was standing knee-deep in the water, just about to launch the fish seaward, when "Snookie" asked me a question I'm sure she regretted later. "Can I have it"?

I tried to explain to her the culinary warnings associated with the little tunny, but she was convinced her husband could make a delight out of it. So, albie in hand, she bounced away in her leopard skin two-piece, popping out in places not meant for the sun. An hour later, John and I headed back to the truck, peering over our shoulders not so much at the skin show, but at the now sun-stroked False Albacore still sunbathing next to the Jersey girls. If they did indeed eat that fish, I hope God had mercy on their digestive systems.

Over the next dozen years, I honed my skills, exploring various shore options, and setting aside vacation time in September and October specifically for chasing albies. My ongoing quest would take me to some of the prettiest coastal regions in southern New England, specifically Massachusetts and Rhode Island. The aforementioned Popponesset Beach region in Mashpee, on Cape Cod was just one in a long list of these locations, and it has yielded many shots from shore, including another time when I made the trek from Oregon Beach in Cotuit, westward towards the Poppy inlet. It was late September, and we were graced with bluebird conditions on the Cape, even as a hurricane was ravaging Florida, bound for the Northeast. Nevertheless, the beautiful weather revealed outstanding visibility as I spied the waters on my walk.

Occasionally pausing at the jetties along the way for a blind cast, and hoping for an unseen target, it wasn't until I just about reached my destination that I saw my first sign of Fat Albert. The pod of albies was way offshore, off the mouth of the Poppy spit, blitzing near the outer red channel marker. I watched the frothing mass, and there could be no doubt… they were following the channel directly towards the inlet. The slashing was getting closer and closer, and before long, the fish were just outside the jetty. My first cast with a 7/8 silver Hogy epoxy jig lasted two cranks of my reel before a silver torpedo attacked. Rather than race into the inlet, the fish left the school and headed down the shoreline for a dogged battle. Blazing through the shallows, there was no quit in this fish, even when it finally beached itself. A quick photo, and I released the albie to rejoin its school.

However, I'd be doing you all a disservice if I didn't speak the truth of albie fishing. It is not easy, especially from shore! I realize from my previous examples it sounds like you just show up, take a couple casts, and ahhh shit… hooked up! Nope, nada, nothing doing.

More often than not, you spend fruitless hours waiting for a sign of fish, or at least for a fish close enough to have a shot. One of my other favorite Cape spots, Woods Hole, aka the gateway to Martha's Vineyard, has seen me burn through numerous hours, sunrise to sunset, with some days never getting a worthwhile shoe. Fish rocketing from the water, teasing me with the possibility of a hookup, while boiling on the surface on the opposite side of the bay. And, when they do show, it may be for literally a matter of seconds, where one cast is all you get. But then you have those days when it all makes it worth it, like one special day a few years ago.

It isn't the quality of the fishing that makes Woods Hole one of my favorite spots to fish. Sure, that's definitely an attraction, but Woods Hole itself is the main draw. It's one of the most picturesque villages on the Cape, with quaint cafés, seaside raw bars, and the funky vibe given off by the scientists rolling through the streets from the Woods Hole Oceanographic Institute and the NOAA laboratory.

The day started as so many others had, with me waking at four a.m., off on another expedition. After getting myself right and prepped, I arrived in the darkness of a mid-September morning before six a.m. and gathered my albie gear. These days, this means two light fishing rods, eight-to-nine-feet, reels spooled with twenty-pound braid, fifteen-pound fluorocarbon leaders, and a small lure bag filled with a handful of jigs and small plastics.

The cool mist was swirling about my head, dotting my exposed skin. The sun would soon be trying to burn through the clouds, and the anticipation was growing as I'd had some success on and off over the last couple of weeks. A fish here, another there, with a lull or two interspersed. They were here; I knew that. That's always the first step. Alert, focused, as the skies brightened I spied the water stretched across the channel toward the green channel marker. Something about that magical green can always gets the first showcase of the day. And when you see that pod of albies mysteriously appear, and turn the water around that can into a boiling pot, you know you have a shot.

Then the waiting game begins anew, until you get your shot. Typically, the fish will work their way around the bay many times throughout the day, but will spend ninety percent of the time under the water, showing no sign on top. Then suddenly… the water explodes with fish slashing, porpoising after baitfish. Peanut bunker, silversides, anchovies, splaying across the water. I readied myself from my perch atop the old stone pier, or what was left of it after the hurricane decades earlier halved it during the storm. Minutes soon turned to hours, and before long, the call of nature and a grumbling in my stomach drew me from my station.

Four hours. Not one fish anywhere near a worthy cast. This is where a lot of anglers fall, taking the dejection, tucking their tails, and retire to other life offerings. But for those with albie fever, it's part of the game. You can make a hundred casts before a hookup, or cast dozens of times into finicky fish before a bite. That's why, unless chasing them from shore, I'll almost always go albie fishing, or more rightly, albie "hunting," solo. And so, on this solo outing, it was time to hit the Pie in the Sky, grab one of their delicious egg & cheese croissants, a cup of coffee, and take a drive along the West Falmouth shoreline to recharge my batteries.

The sun had finally done its job, and was now offset in an early afternoon sky. The warm breeze had a hint of summer to it now, and upon my return to the pier, the few anglers who had shared the jetty with me earlier had all faded into their lives elsewhere. I was alone on a beautiful day, overlooking what appeared to be a placid stretch of water. Honestly, from the morning's results, my hopes were dwindling, but as my close fishing buddies know, I don't give up easily. In other words, "it ain't over until the fat lady sings." And this is why.

My "peaceful easy feeling" was blown wide open as the water exploded mere feet away from me, as a pod of big albies erupted. A perfect cast with a green/silver/orange epoxy hit the note spot on and with two snaps of the lure I came tight. The fish bolted straight for the ferry terminal opposite the small cove I was looking out on. It fought as all little tunnies do, no surrender…all the way to the rocky edge. The fish, easily twelve pounds or more, was brilliant in the sun. Tribal markings, black dots on the belly, green, silver, hues of purple. A masterpiece.

That one fish had made my day, but I didn't know that I was far from done. For the next few hours, pod after pod made their presence known on both sides of the pier, and five fish later, I was prepared to call it a day as it slowed somewhat. I hooked the plastic jig that I had recently switched to, a pink Albie Snax, to an eyelet on my rod, and headed off the jetty, just before I made a fisherman's "mistake." I turned my head back for one last look, and immediately caught the beginning of a renewed blitz straight off the tip of the pier.

Running back to the end of the stones, in haste I launched my lure with an extra push, sending it directly at the wooden piling just off the end. The Albie Snax bounced off the dolphin and splashed down into the middle of a frenzied sea, and was immediately crushed by one last albie. A final reward for sticking out the dead sea of morning!

Poppy Beach and Woods Hole are just two of the areas in the stretch along the Nantucket Sound shoreline from Falmouth to Cotuit that can offer great opportunities for shore albies, but the stretch from Cotuit to Chatham can be just as productive, or even more, during certain seasons. The reality is, the whole run from Chatham to the Cape Cod Canal can be alive with albies any given time of year.

During the season, depending on water conditions, the fish may be blitzing off Hardings Beach in Chatham on one day, the next off Craigville Beach, then Woods Hole, and anywhere in Buzzard's Bay. But for Massachusetts albie anglers, if there can be a guaranteed hotspot, year after year, it has to be the islands. While I haven't really experienced what secrets Nantucket Island carries, the Vineyard is another story. Whether it's the proximity to deeper channels, warmer water eddies from offshore, or other geographical influences, hopping the ferry and answering the call of the islands is hard to resist, for treasures await ye!

This page and following page: Bonito and Albies swarm the inshore waters of Cape Cod every Autumn

Gary Esper, myself, and John Rice with our first Bluefin

Stellwagen Bluefin Tuna on the swimming plug

A Captiva Spinner Shark put on an aerial display and narrowly avoided becoming dinner for a larger specimen, as seen by the teeth marks on its flank

Big Bass rebound in the 90s

The Cape Cod Canal's most famous commuter, the Striped Bass

Captain Terry Nugent puts us on hungry Albies along the Elizabeth Islands

Wire-lining jigs on the Monomoy rips back in the 80s and 90s was a common practice

Perhaps my all-time favorite; topwater jumbo Bluefish!

A Plum Island Jumbo Bass

A healthy Cape Cod Bluefish

Chapter 14

The Silver Bullet Express – Martha's Vineyard

I had been to Martha's Vineyard numerous times over many decades, from family trips as a kid, to couples getaways, and the fishing vibe is always present. Thus, of course, a fishing rod and tackle always finds a place in the truck or trunk. Stripers and blues in Menemsha in the Spring. More bass off State Beach. And then the fall season arrives, and what was a crowded tourist destination swaps its busy tourists for anxious fishermen and women—it's derby time.

I never officially partake in the Martha's Vineyard Striped Bass and Bluefish Derby, as I can never dedicate that much time to the island. But the feel is in the air from the moment you arrive in Woods Hole and prepare to depart from the mainland. Most trips begin with a stop for coffee and croissants at Pie in the Sky bakery, in Woods Hole, unless departing later in the day. Then I recommend you check out some of the cool, coveside spots like Captain Kidd's restaurant for clam chowder, or Shuckers, where Rum Punch and oysters await. Whether a morning or afternoon departure, there's no denying the buzz in the air. Even though we're talking about a short, thirty-minute ferry trip, there's something electric about being up top, watching the Falmouth coast grow distant as gulls cry and the Vineyard gets closer.

The salt air floats on the breeze, the boat rolls gently, and mystery awaits.

My first albie quest to the Vineyard was really a sidenote to a romantic holiday for my beautiful wife, Shannon, and me. Even though I "robbed the cradle," as the saying goes (why the fuck does the saying go like that? A little pervy, if you ask me), with Shannon being eleven years younger than this old salt, we were lucky in that we shared birthdays around the Columbus Day weekend. So we like to try and escape for the weekend. Due to the island's charm, its fishing heritage, and its geography, the Vineyard is one of those places where you can truly do it.

We arrived on a morning ferry. The Island Inn, tucked between Oak Bluffs and Edgartown, had check-in later in the day. Naturally, I had our morning planned out, with a dropping tide expected at Menemsha. A quick stop at the "Our Market" mini-mart for supplies (see beer and snacks), and we were headed west, cutting through the island.

One of the cool things I love about the island is that the movie *Jaws* was filmed here! Yes, *Jaws*! Otherwise known as not only the greatest fishing movie ever put to film, but the greatest movie ever made! Yeah, I might be a bit biased. Well, some of the scenes were filmed in Menemsha, like when Captain Quint's boat the Orca is departing from the harbor to go hunting the Great White Shark. Of course, driving into the village, I had to grace Shannon with my rendition of a sweet poem delivered by Quint in the movie: "Here lies the body of Mary Lee. Died at the age of a hundred n' three. For fifteen years, she kept her virginity. Not a bad record for this vicinity." I just can't resist. But my lovely bride tolerates my quotes day in, day out, and not just Brody's "we're gonna' need a bigger boat," but "Hooper drives the boat Chief," or "What are ya…some kind of half-assed astronaut," and on and on. And when she comes out with a quote on her own? Well, move aside Grinch, my heart grows ten times bigger, and more.

We pulled into the Menemsha lot overlooking the sound and jetty, with the port behind us. First things first, I needed to do some prospecting. Were albies around? I geared up with my small albie bag and rod, and scanned the inlet and east along the beach. No action was noticeable, and nothing west towards Lobsterville Beach, another renowned hotspot. But that's what makes the Vineyard special. It almost didn't matter that the fish weren't there. Yes, I'd caught a variety over the years from this very spot, but the feeling the feeling of calm, of island time, just makes the anxiety fade away. This place is special.

Then there are the sunsets. Throughout the tourist season and into Autumn, folks gather with chairs, towels, couples, kids, whole families, and friends. Wine, cheese, beer, chips. They wait and watch as one of the northeast's most beautiful sunsets creeps closer to the horizon before vanishing into Vineyard Sound. I've witnessed many a sunset from Key West to Captiva, and while the crowds may not be as heavy or rowdy, it may be the most serene ending to a day you ever see.

That day, however, the sun was still high in the sky. Lunch was calling, and Larsen's Fish Market was answering. The world needs more Larsen's and fewer McDonalds. A local family joint that buys fish from the backdoor boats that tie up, Larsen's is, in every sense of the word, a fish market. If you're looking for fancy, move along. With grey-weathered shakes for siding, a swinging screen door, and sea blue accents, this salty shack that has been a welcoming locals and tourists for over fifty years. The few picnic tables outside are the only seating you'll find on site, but nothing tastes better than Larsen's on the beach. Hot-buttered lobster rolls, a cup of chowder, and ice-cold beer to wash it down. What's a little sand in your shorts when you're in heaven?

After lunch, I put the albie quest on hold, not wanting to bore my wife all day with a thousand casts into an empty sea, and decided to do a bit of exploring. The famous lighthouse of Aquinnah was next up. Aquinnah, originally established as Gay Head by settlers, was renamed in years past to honor the original settlers, the Native American tribe of the Wampanoag, and basically translates to "land under the hill." This translation just doesn't do justice to the actual "land under the hill," but understanding the Wampanoag lore for the history of the area gives you an idea. Legend says that a great giant named Moshup dragged his foot from the mainland, creating the islands and the awe-inspiring cliffs of Aquinnah. The red hues of the majestic cliffs were stained red by the blood of whales that Moshup would catch, passing down the knowledge of fishing and catching through the generations for thousands of years. It is said Moshup still keeps watch over the peoples of the island, and I imagined him there as Shannon and I looked out over the lighthouse, the red beacon highlighting the cliffs and turquoise waters.

After some reflecting of nature's beauty before us, it was time to head east, in the direction of our hotel. Our route took us along the coast, where we made a quick stop for a walk and a couple of cold Coronas at Lucy Vincent Beach. If you haven't been to Lucy Vincent, definitely add it to your "must-visit" list when visiting the island. The beach is open only to residents of the town in season, but before June 1st and after Labor Day, it's open for all. Beautiful sand, red clay cliffs, and monoliths on the beach, it is one of the coolest beaches I've ever seen in the Northeast.

And the fishing is decent too. If you get a chance to wet a line, head east on the beach past the big clay boulders. There you'll see a large rock offshore. This piece of real estate holds stripers en masse during the spring. After knocking back a couple of cold ones, we shook the sand from our shoes and continued cross island. Our return trip brought us upon the funky sculpture garden called the Field Gallery, in West Tisbury. There is a definite artist's vibe across the island, along with many galleries, but this is definitely one to check out if you get a chance. The stark white, dancing sculptures in the grass were just what we needed as the clouds started to roll in. Eventually, we found our way back to the Island Inn before heading into Oak Bluffs for a cocktail at the Ritz, followed by dinner at the Wharf Pub in Edgartown.

The next morning, we awoke to a slight drizzle—a perfect day to go albie hunting! My plan started with a stop for breakfast goods and coffee, and then off to the OnTime ferries to Chappaquiddick. Surprisingly, there were only a few cars in line at the Edgartown launch, which was fine by me. I figured it must be the wet weather, but either way, we were off on a new quest. If you're not familiar with the Chappy ferry, the trip takes just a few minutes, as the expanse is perhaps a couple football fields in length. Of course, if you've seen the greatest fishing movie in history, you'll see the ferry in a scene where Chief Brody is confronted by the Mayor about closing the beach.

Once across, we headed along the road towards East beach. The pavement eventually morphs into a dirt road as you near our first stop, Wasque Point, on the southeast tip of the Vineyard. Wasque is almost just as stunning as the aforementioned Lucy Vincent Beach, with a breathtaking seascape, cliffs, and an expanse of open sand and sea. A great rip sets off from the point, and from spring through summer, into fall, fishermen ferry over or drive the sand and set up for the day. Vacationing adventurers in their 4x4s abandon the crowds of the main part of the island for an otherworldly escape.

That day, however, my stomach turned as the ocean came into view. A frothing, mad sea was at work. Towering waves, whitecaps being ripped and whipped by the wind. There would be no fishing here today. Shannon and I put our raincoats on and made a dash for the beach, if only to give her an introduction to this vast wonderland. Plan B was up next. A short jaunt to the northeast corner lead us to

UNTIL THE NEXT TIDE

the Cape Poge Gut. The gut is a narrow inlet into Cape Poge Bay, and can be loaded with albies and bonito, as can be said about most corners of the island. However, with the tumultuous seas to the south driven by the wind, I knew this area would be protected from the weather. I pulled into the small lot at the reserve and, after a brief talk with a couple of fly fishermen exiting the lot, my hopes were renewed. There were a few anglers down along the shore of the gut, but neither the fly guys nor the others had hooked up. However, False Albacore were showing, teasing the fishermen with boiling water, while refusing their offerings.

Shannon and I buttoned up, and I grabbed my gear. Heading down the steep stairs that overlook the inlet, I decided to head north where no other anglers were set up. It appeared as though they were concentrating on the inner part of the inlet. This might have been for good reason, as the tide was coming in and dumping into the bay. This was my first time at the gut, and also Derby time, but I could clearly see signs of fish closer to the open ocean, and not a soul working that direction. We moved past a couple fishing near the bottom of the stairs and waded down the shore until I was almost in casting range. I was just short in my casts across the whole of the inlet, and after changing my light lure to a one-ounce Hogy peanut bunker jig, I was in the zone.

Three casts later, I was tight. The albie fought incredibly hard in the current, racing down the shoreline with me in chase trying to keep up and not break him off. When I wrapped my hand around the tail of a ten-pound albie, the anglers nearby offered congratulations. Partial grimaces and furrowed brows would follow after I told them I wasn't entered into the derby, as I released the fish. With conditions worsening, it was an easy choice to call this quest a success and head for the ferry.

It was after noontime when we drove off the ferry into Edgartown, and there was only one spot in mind. With it being Sunday, typically we'd be looking for a place for the Patriots game, but it was a bye week. Either way, it was NFL gameday, and the best place around for Bloody Marys, chowder, Buffalo wings and multiple games was right around the corner, the Seafood Shanty. The rain was steady now, but it was relatively warm, and the topside bar had the doors open to the deck out back. The crowd was lively, the service was top notch, and the food and drink… right on. An occasional mist would blow in from the open deck, but nothing could dampen my spirits. I had my sweetheart by my side, and had landed an albie in uncertain conditions, in a place I had never fished before. Man, life was indeed good!

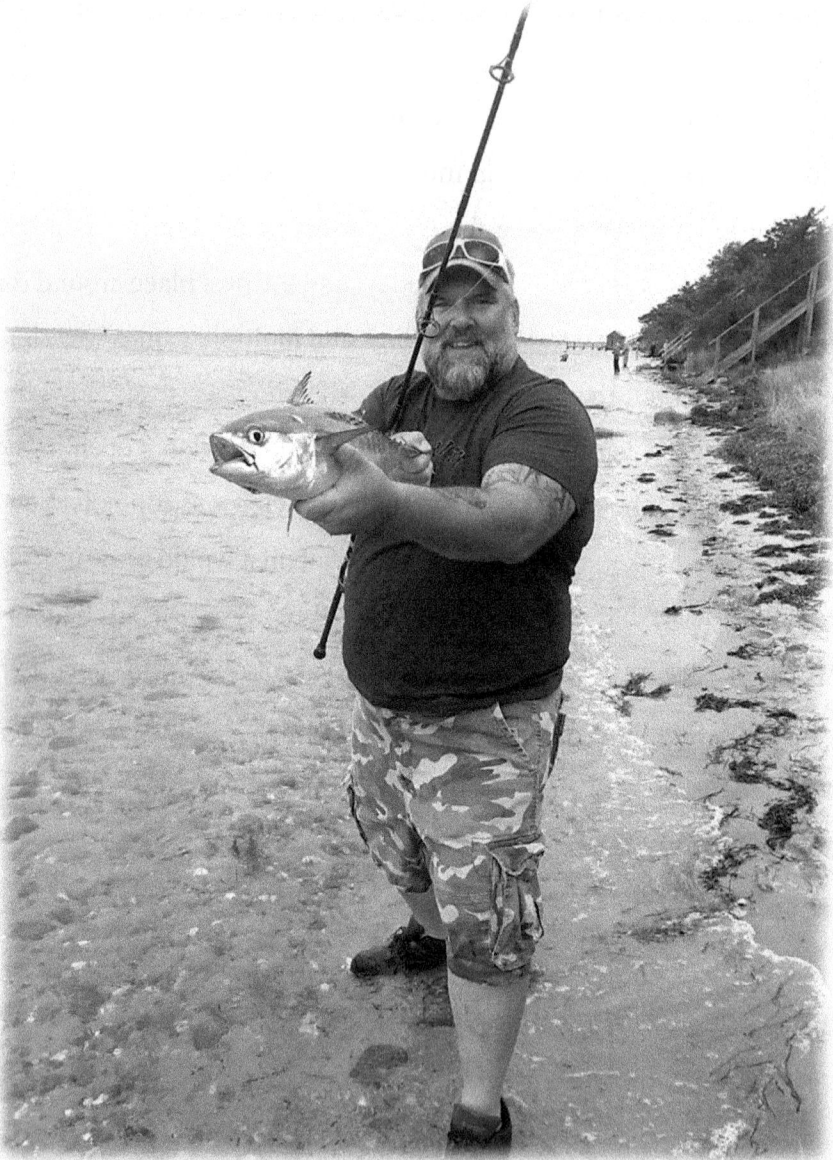

A hard-charging Chappaquiddick False Albacore

Chapter 15

The Silver Bullet Express – Rhode Island

Recent years have seen me exploring other locales outside the Bay State—Rhode Island, to be precise. The smallest state in the Union isn't called the Ocean State for nothing, and its proximity to the fertile waters of Buzzards Bay, Narragansett Bay, and nearby Long Island Sound is like a magnet for little tunny. Many moons had passed since John and I encountered that fish off the East Wall of Point Judith, and I actually had an idea of what I was doing. Over the years the *quahog telegraph* had given up a few secrets and tips on hotspots, which I'm sure some of you will be less than thrilled with me for including in this tome. It's somewhat funny, given that so many of us learned of spots from weekly reports printed in various periodicals throughout the years. As a matter of fact, I distinctly recall reading of famous locales such as the West Well of Point Jude, and Watch Hill, where fish-tales of silver speedsters played out. The funny part is, as a kid, so many of these reports influenced me to pick up a surf rod, and leave the known commodity of sweetwater haunts. Places like Sakonnet Point, where the open Atlantic converges with Buzzards Bay. The jetty at the point is relatively well known these days, with diehard regulars who stake claim in the early hours of every day during albie season, and for good reason. The albie fishing here can be hot and heavy, and some years you'll have a legitimate shot at cracking double digits. The bonus here is, it can be quite a Bonito spot in addition to the Fat Alberts.

Of course, albies can be unpredictable from year to year, and environmental conditions, from late season storms, temperature and water clarity, can dictate what kind of season we'll have, or how long it will last; so it pays to have options. When I first started exploring the area, one of the key tools in my arsenal was a map. I would study the shoreline, the coves, the drop-offs and deep holes. This is what led me to South County R.I. This stretch of southerly facing shoreline basically runs from Point Judith to Watch Hill, and is interspersed with salt ponds that all dump into the sound.

The Charlestown, Quonnie, and Weekapaug breachways see a lot of foot traffic for good reason. Bass, blues, and albies can all be had here, quality and quantity. I typically prefer the beaches in between the breachways when looking for albies; and I'd like to say it's to avoid the crowds, more than anything else. The reality is, I'd rather spread out on these stunning stretches of sand than rub elbows with weekend warriors tossing three-ounce pencil poppers at a school of little tunny.

The Narragansett shoreline was my point of origin for a recent quest, starting near the pier, and a well-known location at the tip of Hazard Avenue, called "Hazard Rock." The spectacular rocky shoreline here is not only beautiful, but as its name reveals, can also be dangerous, especially in rough conditions. Many fishermen have been swept off the rocks, seriously injured or taken to Davey Jones' locker; so, it is well-advised to keep away during *hazardous* conditions.

The rocks along this stretch see their fair share of bait fishermen in search of Scup, Black Sea Bass, and Tautog. Large bass and blues also provide great action for plugging and bait guys. But, come September, albies and bonito can show in force all down the rocky shoreline, enticed by the deep, and sudden drop-offs along the ledges. I arrived at sunrise, stretched my cleats over my sneakers, and worked my way over the rocks to the edge of the rocks. The first pods were already visible offshore, on a sunny morning with outstanding visibility. I could literally see for miles, and as the minutes ticked away, more and more pods of happy albies were spotting the surface with white water. Then, to my left, the albies exploded right in close. A flyrodder was in perfect position, and hooked up immediately. I anxiously waited and watched as the fish disappeared below the ripples, and seconds later, a splash a few short yards directly in front of me guided my cast.

The take was vicious as the fish turned on it after just a couple of cranks of the reel. My line sizzled from my Shimano reel, as the little tunny bolted right, and in an instant, left. I cautiously stepped down the decline, avoiding the slick, black rocks, and played the waves, timing the crest to slide my fish onto the smooth ledge. The next hour saw fish caught from all points within my vision, onshore and offshore, as the center console brigade joined the fun. Some time later, a lull in the action turned into only an occasional splash. A swing and a miss, and a hope the tide change later in the day would get the fish moving again, after the tide let up.

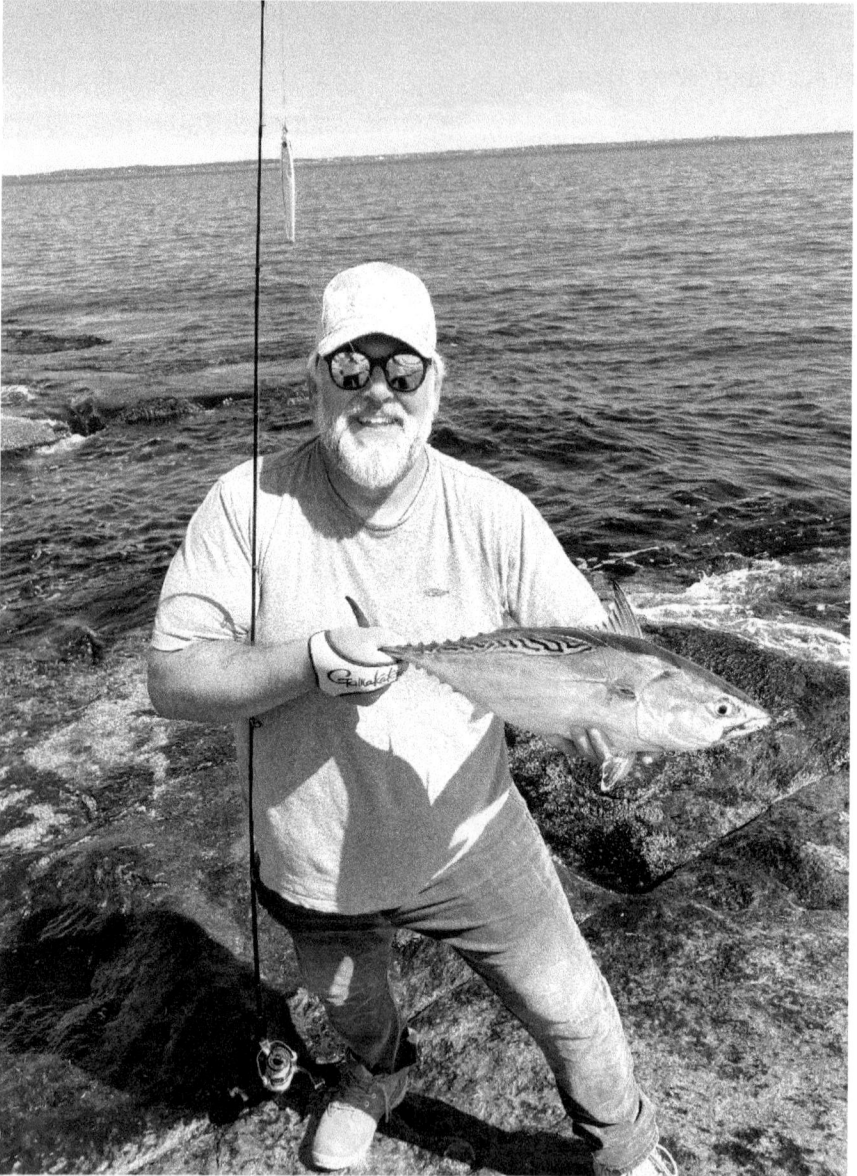

I had one last trick in my book, which well-known Cape Cod charter guide, Captain Warren Marshall introduced me to years before. I tied on a seven-to-eight-inch Hogy epoxy jig directly to my 20lb braid, removed the hook, and added a two-foot stretch of leader material. On the business end, I tied on a small, sand eel fly. Casting out the jig, I let it sink slightly, and then worked it back such as you would a streamer fly, short and quick snaps of the jig.

The albie that crushed it sped off down the shoreline, whipping my line in an arc over the surface of the water, throwing a spray that was illuminated in rainbow fashion. After what was one of my most memorable shore-caught albies, the action completely flamed out, and it was time to explore further westward, along the South County shoreline.

Since it was still relatively early, late morning, I decided to make the run almost to the Connecticut border, to the village of Watch Hill. The reports had detailed blitzing False Albacore, and my plan was to fish my way around the historic lighthouse and spot check the coastline on an afternoon return trip to Narragansett. Plus, maybe, just maybe, I'll spot Taylor Swift about town, if she ventures out from her massive mansion on near East Beach. While that would be kinda cool, my focus was on the boats working the pods of albies visible around the parking lot and the lighthouse.

Watch Hill isn't the easiest place to navigate around the rocky shore, but the pods were scattered and you could move plenty of times and still have a chance fish would pop up. Blind casting as I made way around the west side of the peninsula, the silver bullet express hit the jig so quickly that my rod was nearly pulled out of my hand. After a TV show release (I grabbed the leader as the albie popped off the line), the next half hour had my head on swivel. A splash to the left. A dozen to the right. The frothing appeared to be migrating more towards the east side of the lot, so I followed, hoping for another shot.

Just at the bend of the parking lot, nearing the exit, I came tight but immediately popped off. Bad luck and superstition had me back in my truck, heading east, 0-2 in Watch Hill albies, and 0-0 in Taylor sightings. I checked out the lots and beaches from Misquamicut to Charlestown, opting to skip the oft-crowded and known albie hotspot of the West Wall in Point Judith, returning to the morning's rocky ledges. Kicking myself for not sticking it out in Narragansett was easy, as the albies were putting on a late day blitz and gifted me with one last fish.

These days, Narragansett and South County are a regular part of the rotation, and the area makes a great destination for Indian Summer days with the family, or a couples getaway, with a few casts followed up with drinks at George's of Galilee and dinner at the Matunuck Oyster Bar. There's nothing quick like watching the sunset reflect off the currents of the salt pond from their rooftop tables. And the oyster stew! Oh, sweet baby Jesus!

Chapter 16

Ocean Awash the Gunwale

If you haven't quite figured it out yet, I tend to lean more towards the surfcasting legion, with waders, surfbags, and long sticks to tempt the denizens of the deep with faux offerings. But many a trip has also been spent atop the waves, and not along the edge of sand. I've been out on small boats, big boats, and kayaks to offshore party vessels, on flat ass calm days, on raging, mad seas, and everything in between.

My latest on-the-water excursion was courtesy of a trip with Riptide Charters, on Captain Terry Nugent's center console. On our round trip from Monomoy to the Elizabeth Islands, totaling 140 miles chasing albies, we finally found hungry fish around Robinson's Hole, south of Woods Hole. Digging into the archives, my earliest memories of deep sea fishing featured rolling party boats, with cod and haddock the targets, and my brother Chris and me barely able to see over the rail. My late teens and twenties found me and my buddies dipping our toes into the deep blue. John, Gary, Mike, and I, along with the occasional scattering of other long-haired tradesmen, would save and consolidate our funds to book charters every year. Dreams of trophy Striped Bass would bring us to Saquatucket Harbor, Harwich, and Cape Cod, numerous times over the years, bound for the rich waters off Monomoy island and the Nantucket Shoals, where the most highly regarded method of the day was ripping wire line with lead head jigs, or trolling hoochies through the rips.

For us, it was a day off the ladder or the staging, and a chance to possibly catch some giant bass and Bluefish, while crushing beers and good-hearted jabs. Usually, we'd end each trip with a boatload of fish and sore rips from all the laughs. Captains like Bob Luce, with his boat the "Striper," would put us on the fish with no need for modern electronics. I swear that guy could smell the fish, and taught us a lot about jigging wire. I believe good old Bob left this earth sometime around 2012, but he made a lasting impact for those who fished with him—at least I know he did for us.

Then there was a gent named Captain Tom Szado, who, at the time, ran and owned a charter boat out of the same port, called the "Arlee X," If I'm not mistaken, I'm pretty sure the boat used to be called the "Arlee," until after his divorce. We made several trips with Tom as well, including one particularly memorable excursion to the Nantucket Shoals. For those not familiar with the shoals, the area is a shallow, rippling stretch of sandy fingers off the eastern side of Nantucket Island, close to the shipping lanes. It's a place historically known for being treacherous for wayward ships, resulting in many a wreck. However, the same strong currents that continually transform the shoals also create rips and drop-offs that fish such as bass, blues, and Fluke find irresistible. They create the perfect ambush structure to attack disoriented baitfish and squid, so of course Captain Tom liked to take his charters there.

We had fished these very waters on calm days, where the rips followed the contour of the shoals one after the other, producing a slight crest of white water for hundreds of yards in a line, followed by another, and then another. We would work the edge, allowing the current to swing our jigs into the curl of the wave, and watch in awe as big bass and blues could be seen streaking thru the blue-green glass-like wall of the wave, before they erupted on the bait.

Then there were days where it wasn't so calm, one of which I'll never forget. A sunny and warm, yet windy, late summer day, had us on the stern of the Arlee X, working the wall of waves, which were quite substantial compared to the calm days. Huge Bluefish in the high teens were shredding our lures. Distracted by the yellow-eyed devils in hot pursuit, while playing the deck dance of avoiding tangled lines and big fish, none of us had realized we were drifting into a sheer cliff of water, towering over our heads.

As the wave came crashing down upon us, the boat was thrown port-side, almost parallel to the angry sea. No longer were tangled lines a concern; we were all thrown against the freeboard, sprawled against the inside of the hull. Somehow, the Captain was able to crawl to the wheel, punch the throttle, and right the vessel as we plowed through the rip. I don't know if it was the fish gods, Poseidon, or Neptune, but someone was watching out for us that day, as we all stayed in the boat, and eventually made it back to the dock. That wouldn't be our last bass and blue charter, as the bug was sinking in. The need to seek out deeper waters, bigger fish, exotic fish, big water cousins to the pelagics inshore. Tuna? Mahi-Mahi? We were ready to find out.

One of our first trips to deep water was aboard the previously noted charter boat, the "Sea Hawk," out of Galilee, Rhode Island. Reports told of a fantastic tuna bite offshore at the Mud Hole, and conditions were set for an early morning launch. Captain Nick Butziger met us at the dock, as we loaded our gear and headed out in the dark. The burn of a cigarette's ember glowed eerily, coffee steam added to the mist, and the motors hummed as Gary, John, and I settled in for a long ride.

An orange slice on the horizon greeted us as we approached the fleet. Some boats were at anchor, chunking butterfish for tuna. We witnessed one boat which already had a large Yellowfin Tuna hanging from the side. Others were setting up their spreads for the morning troll. We anxiously joined the latter, putting out a six-rod spread, with feather jigs and daisy chains. We knew within a matter of minutes that this wasn't a mere boat ride, as two rods in the spread were knocked down and we were instantly hooked. Doubles, triples, and quadruple hookups were the norm for most of the morning, and when the tide slowed up, it was time for lunch (at ten a.m.). With 'dem bellies full, we were back on the troll.

I was below deck, hittin' the head, when I heard a frantic scramble on deck. We were covered up! All six rods were pinned with tuna infused chaos! The rest of the trip essentially followed the same pattern. Multiple hookups of football Bluefin and Yellowfin Tuna, and even a few albies and bonitio thrown in for good measure. Simply an outstanding day for numbers, and tasty, peppercorn tuna steaks to come. The following year, our trip was lost to the weather, but our appetites for bluewater adventures couldn't be quelled, and the next year, we looked towards the Canyons.

The northeast canyons, for those unaware of the offshore geography, are an area where the continental shelf plummets to incredible depths. Picture the Grand Canyon covered by a few hundred feet of water. That is essentially the gulfstream highway, following the edge of the wall of the continental shelf where the bottom drastically drops from perhaps three hundred feet to thousands of feet deep. The canyons are just that, splinters in the wall of the shelf, with the edge beginning approximately ninety to one hundred miles south of New England.

The water depth from the islands gradually deepens from approximately one hundred to three hundred feet, until the bottom drops out. Here, the gulf currents sweep upward, bringing nutrients and all sorts of aquatic creatures and baitfish, with tropical species like tuna, marlin, Mahi-Mahi, and Wahoo on the hunt, allowing northeast anglers an opportunity that most presume only exists in southern waters.

Canyons such as Veatch, Atlantis, and Hydrographers are typical targets for bluewater jockeys in our area. Additionally, warm water eddies will spin off throughout the summer and fall, bringing these hot pockets with the pelagics in tow, much closer to the mainland, occasionally just twenty miles south of Martha's Vineyard, and other places like the Mud Hole to the west.

When planning a trip to the canyons, the commitment is serious for both charters and crew, but also for recreational sportfishermen in their own vessels, and the cost is substantial to cover bait, fuel, and time, as it can take many hours to get there. If your target is indeed an actual canyon, and not a closer warm water eddy, it is not unreasonable to depart at midnight expecting to be arriving to your target location for sunrise. There are many dark hours during which sleep, if possible, will help pass the time, but when you arrive and the skies begin to lighten, the world changes into something so beautiful you have to see it to understand.

Our first journey east to the canyons, sometime in the mid-to-late nineties, saw Mike, John, and me stepping aboard a thirty-three-foot Blackfin sportfisher, docked at the Falmouth Harbor marina, just below the Flying Bridge restaurant. The misty glow around the dock lights painted an eerie backdrop, highlighted by the cranky prick who skippered the boat. The Captain seemed more annoyed than eager to venture offshore, and the stale whiskey on his breath seeped from his rotten lips as we pushed off. Whether he was nursing a hangover, or spiked his coffee, I can't say, but at least we stayed above the water for duration of our trip. If I could remember his name, I'd surely call him out. For now, let's just call him Captain Shithead.

We reached the edge of the canyon just after dawn broke, greeted by a pod of whales and porpoises. The morning troll produced one knockdown, but not much after, until we set up to chum and drift. The tuna bite proved to be non-existent, at least where we were setup. After many hours spent getting there, and the hard-earned dollars we paid, we were anxious for action. We asked about checking the offshore lobster pots for Mahi-Mahi, and Captain Shithead agreed. Hopping from pot to pot is a well-known strategy when looking for mahi, as some can have zero life on them, and then you come up on one that is covered up with bait and predators. These green, glowing, zigzagging, blunt-headed sportfish not only look amazing, but taste delicious.

The third pot we came upon, on the edge of the canyon and in hundreds of feet of water, was covered up with the fish of many names—dorado in Mexico, dolphinfish in Florida, and Mahi-Mahi in the Pacific. These days, they're mostly referred to as mahi wherever you travel. Captain Shithead cut the butterfish we had for bait into chunks and started chumming, and the fish immediately responded. Burying a hook into a chunk and free-lining it into the chum brought immediate results, and we spent the rest of the trip filling the boat with green and yellow mahi, fins all lit-up blue. The three of us bailed the fish, the majority being "chicken-sized" in the three-to-found pound range, with a few nearing ten pounds.

With constant double and triple hook-ups, there were mostly smiles all around. I say "mostly" because at one point, Mike and John had to cool me down as I was hot at whiskey breath. We had been on the deck of many a charter boat by this time and knew the safety protocols and how to interact. Yet Captain Shithead wouldn't let us all the way to the stern of the boat! Completely ridiculous. We all knew the dance around the deck; but it was his delivery that got me steamed. He has no idea how close he came to going for a swim.

The long ride back allowed me to decompress, take a snooze, and have a couple of beers with my mates, and by the time we stepped off the dock, the smiles had returned as we looked forward to the tasty, fresh mahi fillets that would soon grace the grill.

A couple of years later, we were ready to give it another go. The craving for a return to the canyons had us pooling our money. John and Mike were onboard for another adventure, but Captain Shithead was long-ago written off. We sought out an experienced, reliable, mild-mannered dude, and Captain Shawn Ozolins fit the bill perfectly. I didn't know it at the time of booking, but Shawn was also an alum of Marian High School. The "Reaction" was a well-equipped sportfisher, comfortable ride, and together with his wife Kelly, his "mate" on deck and off, they made for a perfect crew. I can't recall where we left from, I think possibly Hyannis, but we pushed off the dock just after midnight, with a six-hour cruise ahead of us.

We inched closer to the edge as the black skies turned to a milky orange. As the sun fought the darkness, eventually winning with broken rays rippling atop the relatively flat surface, something lay just ahead. It was a bit difficult to make out at first, as the dawn was still adjusting in our eyes. But soon, there was no mistaking what we were looking at. A large sickle tail of a White Marlin, trailing a slight disturbance. We called to Captain Shawn, who was manning the wheel from atop the tower, just as the big fish twisted hard and dove, leaving a circle of whitewater behind.

The skipper spun the wheel and we readied some trolling lures, wishing we had live eels or other baitfish that would tempt the marlin.

After about twenty minutes, it was clear the fish was either gone or not interested in what we had to offer, but still, what a sight to break the morning light. We continued trolling as with our initial canyon excursion, and had a couple hits, with school tuna hitting the deck. Once again, spotty action eventually sent us in search of high-flyers, also known as the offshore lobster pots, and the fish we hoped would be underneath.

At this point in my salty history, I thought I could handle anything with a surf rod, so it was only natural, at least to me, to stow a nine-foot surf rod with a Penn 5500 reel and twenty-pound mono, in case the chance arose for a cast at mahi. Not the smartest decision I've ever made.

The sun was high now, giving Shawn a clean view into the purple, super clear water, and the unmistakable hues of large Mahi-Mahi. As we passed, I asked if I could make a cast with my surf rod, with a 1.5 ounce Storm shad lure hanging from the business end. "Let it rip," he called out, and that's exactly what I did. My cast was right on the money, nearly hitting the high-flyer reflectors, splashing down right at the base.

Two cranks in, and a massive hit and hookup had my drag screaming. "Big bull" was heard from behind me, as a huge male mahi broke the surface. The fish must've jumped thirty straight times, trying to throw the lure. If you've never seen a bull mahi, it is easily recognized by its squared-off blunt head, compared to the more rounded head of the female of the species, and typically much larger. This fish was showing me who was boss, especially on my surf outfit.

However, the give and take finally slowed, as I pressured the fish to the side of the boat. Kelly was standing alongside, gaff in hand, and when the fish was just off starboard, she went in to stick him. The sigh of relief I was just beginning to let out quickly went the other way, as the gaff bounced off its flanks, and the mahi screamed towards the depths.

At this point, I'm not how deep we were, but one hundred yards spilled from my reel in seconds. John and Mike, yelling words of encouragement, had me more determined than ever, and I was moved to break one of the cardinal rules amongst fishermen. I tightened the drag slightly, hoping to gain more of an advantage in the battle. "Don't touch the drag" is a phrase that all experienced anglers have heard their whole lives, and I wish I'd listened to that little voice in the back of my mind. The thirty-pound leader parted shortly thereafter, the fish's sandpaper teeth finally chaffing though. A mahi over thirty pounds doesn't show up on the end of a surf-rod very often, but the loss was made less painful by a handful of teen-sized to twenty-pound Mahi-Mahi that followed. A far better quality of fish than our first canyon adventure.

While the lure of the canyons and the mysteries that await offshore can certainly attract the adventurous, the expeditions come at a price, including sleeplessness, sore shoulders, and damage in the wallet. Private charters can range from the low thousands to well over two thousand for overnighters. Even if you can gather a few salty souls to commit, it's still a dent in the ol' savings jug. But fear not, fellow fishers, for many ports from here to Jersey offer party boats trips that, while without the privacy of your own charter, can still put you on the exotic species found in the bluest of waters.

One of our favorite outfits we book is out of Hyannis, on Cape Cod. The Helen H has a few big boats under their parent name, with excursions for Black Sea Bass, Fluke, Cod, and offshore tuna. Party boat fishing is the perfect option for family trips, shorter days, with the camaraderie between the rails, where daily regulars swap tales, with Grandpa taking his grandkids out for their first trip. Of course, you always get a couple of sharpies who keep everything close to the vest, but having a good time is always at the heart of these trips, offering a spacious cabin area to escape nasty weather, tables to take a break for lunch, and restroom facilities. The tuna trips take this to the next level. You'll have a few newbies here and there, but for the most part, you have men and women who know what they're looking for: Tuna, possibly Mahi, maybe a Mako Shark, and if the fishing gods are shining, even a swordfish.

John and I joined a group of fishermen early one morning, about six a.m., waiting anxiously on the dock, taking stock in our equipment, and preparing to board the Helen H. The one-hundred-foot super cruiser was prepping for a five-to-six-hour steam to the northeast canyons, what would be the beginning of a two-day trip, targeting mostly Yellowfin and Longfin Albacore Tuna, and other pelagics. Rolling our gear onto the ramp, and then down the rail, we settled on a homebase spot on the starboard side, closer to the pulpit than the stern, ahead of midship. Stowing our cooler under the bench, which did include a twelve-pack of Budweiser, but more importantly, turkey sandwiches, water, and snacks, we began readying our tackle.

The beer, of course, was more for the return journey, as we had business at hand, and there would hopefully be little time for suds. We were hitting up the mates for tips on how to approach the afternoon. While we weren't exactly newbies to the offshore scene, the party boat business has its own strategy and standards. The day would start with trolling a nine or ten rod spread off the stern, and the twenty-five anglers were assigned a number system, rotating every twenty minutes from rod one, rod two, rod three, and so on. Certainly, this is a fair way to give everyone a chance at a "hot corner," but the more intriguing strategy was instilled where the stern slows after a bite on the troll, or multi hook-up. When this happens, the mates hit the side of the boat up-current, and start to chum, scooping a slurry of baitfish over the rail, which then keeps the fish in a frenzy, feeding mode.

The midday August sun was directly overhead, and the humid air made an otherwise comfortable-but-warm day a bit sticky. The diesels chugged, laying down the soundtrack for the afternoon, and it seemed like only minutes after the spread was set that the motors eased to slow purr. Fish on! Neither John nor I was on the spread for this first go-around, but nevertheless, seeing that first Yellowfin hit the deck got us amped up. A few more tuna, a mix of yellows and longfin, soon joined the first visitor on ice, and a few ticks of the clock later, John was up and hooked up. A nice longfin came onboard with a gaff tattoo of John's name. I was stoked to add to the icebox myself, but my twenty-minute window came and went without a knockdown and I retreated to homebase to await my next shot.

There were a few pods of fishermen to cycle thru, and I knew I had time to kill. I hadn't paid much attention to the few anglers at the bow spread out on the pulpit, and the engines slowed again. The Helen H's top-notch mates hit the rails, spraying chum into the current. The anglers up front had dropped their lures, four-to-six-ounce flutter jigs, and let them sink a few fathoms before furiously working them up. One fellow hooked up instantly, followed by another. The engines kicked in, and calls of lures up echoed as we went back on the troll.

Quickly, I surveyed my gear. We armed ourselves with two heavy duty spinning rods rigged and ready with Shimano butterfly and Williamson jigs. We stowed our heavy Penn outfits out of the way, and before we knew it, the engines slowed, and opportunity was at hand.

John and I found that the pulpit had thinned out, and we easily had room to establish our footing, quickly dropping our jigs into the melee. Peering into the clear, purple-tinted Gulf waters, we could see tuna slicing through the chum slick. Pumping my spinning rod, and coordinating and dancing my jig, maybe four cranks was all it took, and my rod doubled over. The thirty-pound class fought hard as my hook found purchase, doing its best to avoid the gaff in tightening circles before coming over the rail. No sooner had my fish come to the gaff, when John came tight to his own, a cookie-cutter replica to the tuna I had just caught.

Another chance at the stern had us on smaller Yellowfin during a shift on the troll, and then back to the pulpit to get us back on our jigging game. The trip had been almost perfect to that point. While not giants, we were catching decent, pelagic fish, good weather, and were now hooked up again on the jigs, with more tuna under the bow!

I intentionally note *almost* perfect to that point because of a few shady characters who apparently were more interested in mischief that fishing.

After the latest round of longfin bloodied the deck, we took a short break, as it was worth a cold Bud to celebrate. At this point, we decided to do a quick inventory check, and scoped out our heavy outfits we had tucked into rod holders near the front of the boat. John and I had matching Penn Squall lever drag heavy reels for bigger tuna or swordfish, connected to Reel Easy acid-wrapped offshore rods. Capable enough for brutes, but not quite giant tuna. Regardless, we were ready to drop squid into the depths when the sun dropped, or so I expected. But when we turned our attention back to our rigs, John's rod was where he pinned it, but mine had disappeared. No doubt some shithead had decided to play games, maybe thinking I would forget where I put it. Well, with increasingly louder f-bombs, I searched the boat, and magically made my rod and reel reappear. When I wheeled back around the front of the boat, there it was.

As heated as I was, I was mainly glad to have the rig back, and John and I settled back to homebase for another cold one. Surprise, surprise. Earlier, when we stopped for our first beer, a dude dressed in a dirty polo shirt and his toothless, meth junkie girlfriend asked us if we had an extra beer. Of course, we said no. You don't spend hundreds of dollars per person to go on these trips and forget to bring a cooler with your own refreshments. We didn't actually see the scumbag take anything, but the culprits helped themselves and we were down a few extra beers because of it. The reality of it was, while losing a few beers isn't a big deal, the rotting element of it made it stink even worse. I suppose we should've known better, and kept a closer watch on our supplies. He may even have been the one responsible for taking my fishing rig; and he didn't even appear to be fishing!

Regardless, we were onboard, had caught a few fish that were now sleeping in the icebox, and we were ready for the pasta dinner the crew was preparing in the galley. Swapping our spinning rods for the heavy rigs, John and I stationed our outfits a few feet from each other, opting to stagger the rigs with one just off the bottom and one halfway up. We were anchored just off the edge of the canyons in approximately three-hundred-and-fifty feet, and had sent whole squid down in the hunt for big tuna or swords.

Unfortunately, the first half of the evening was a dud. By midnight, no fish had paid anyone a visit, and we were ready for a bit of shuteye. For the diehard overnighters this would be taboo. They would be unwilling to take the chance of missing the opportunity if the bite turned. But we were exhausted. The galley had a handful of bunks stacked, with many more belowdecks. We opted for the galley, close to our stations, and let sleep creep in. Sometime after midnight, I think around two a.m., the sound of a fish flopping on deck creaked my eyelids open. I saw a big Mahi-Mahi going crazy on the deck, sliding down past the galley door. We climbed from our bunks, baited up our stations again, and hoped for a late night bite.

Mr. Sandman had other plans. I fought off the urge to abandon the rail for a good hour or so, but eventually we gave in to sleep, this time heading below deck. The diesels were humming loud, and the bunks were more plywood than comfort, but the rhythmic churning of the motors sent us into a deep sleep. We only woke when the motors fired up in preparation for the morning troll.

The smell of bacon and pancakes masked the fish and diesel, and we chatted with the other groggy dudes about the night's events. Amazingly, the scramble on deck of a one-hundred-seventy-five-pound Mako Shark hadn't been loud enough to wake us, but it did get the fishing fever revved up as we went back on the troll. The rest of the morning saw a similar outcome to the previous afternoon. Some tuna on the troll, and tuna on the jigs, but nothing gargantuan. Overall, the trip was enough to inspire future trips for sure, and Captain Joe and the crew were outstanding, setting the bar for future party boat trips. Oh, and scumbag and the junkie even left us a few beers for our trip back to port!

Chapter 17

Bluefins, Humpbacks, and Pyrates

Just about the time the call of the Canyons had piqued my interest in the bluewater, my friend Matt Zajac had been drawn to the waters east of Chatham on Cape Cod. For many years, Matt and I would surfcast the great outer beaches from Provincetown to Chatham, and on the southside of Nantucket Sound, slaying huge stripers along the way, especially drifting swimming plugs in Chatham inlet. He had a perfect home base, too; his grandparents had a house just up the street from Harding's Beach near Stage Harbor, Chatham.

Most fishing trips either started or ended with a stop at the Chatham Squire, a local watering hole decorated in old license plates from near and far, with cold beer served up by pretty girls. This was just one of the local haunts where fish tales were swapped, and plans were hatched to make dreams come true. For Matt, one of these dreams had already come true. His Dad had a sweet, twenty-one-foot boat. You know the saying, *a friend with a boat is better than owning a boat?* I'm not sure I buy into that, but here was this Parker Walkaround, anxious to leave a wake in the Atlantic. It was a perfect fishing vessel, durable for making excursions to the rips, and with a nice dry cockpit to escape the early morning mist.

These striper trips usually started with a stop to jig up some squid, hitting the docks inside Stage Harbor, where we would load up. Some nights we'd follow-up with a stop at Chatham inlet to ply the dropping tide. Other days, we'd hit the holes off Harding's and soak some squid for the big spring/early summer bass. And then there were days we'd launch from Ryder's Cove, sunrise and out to the waters just east of Monomoy island. Matt had the gear and had these waters dialed in, and we would scan the depths until we came across that big red ball on the fish finder. Down would go the jigs and sandeel imitations, and the bass would soon be coming over the rail.

Soon, though, drawn by a new challenge, Matt turned his sights to waters just a bit further offshore. Bluefin Tuna were the behemoths among their other tuna cousins. A fish of legend, with legit *granders* caught every year from Canada to the Northeast. The world record was for a 1,496 pound monster caught off Nova Scotia in 1979, perhaps a record that will forever stand the test of time. But nonetheless, a dream shared by all big game fishermen.

For Matt, his target would hopefully be a fish in the hundreds of pounds, but the thing about Bluefin? The recreational-sized fish—fish from footballs of twenty to sixty pounds or more—these fish don't know they're small. They don't give an inch, and will make you work for it. Some days, you get fish measured in inches. Some days you get fish measured in pounds. Matt has caught them all. The day that he first invited me to join him on a tuna trip just east of Chatham, I knew we would catch, but didn't know what to expect.

That day, trolling spreader bars, squid bulbs bubbling on the surface, had tuna regularly crashing the spread, with doubles of football-sized fish. Nothing topping a hundred pounds, but the sheer power of these fish amazed me. I had nothing to compare it with, although giant Tarpon in the Florida Keys came close. A couple more outings for Bluefin would leave me with sore shoulders and a yearning for battles yet to come. A foggy number of years would pass, surfcasting always taking center stage—stripers, Bluefish, albies—until one day, my friend Gary told me had an investor ready to back his treasure salvage expedition on the north shore of Boston. Part of this included the purchase of a thirty-five-foot downeaster lobster boat. Soon, the boat would undergo a transformation in preparation for the coming season.

Of course, in addition to the sand blowers, mailboxes that covered the props to help remove sand from the bottom, dry suits and scuba tank holders, this also meant rod holders and outriggers. With little fanfare, other than a dockside toast, the "Sea Tek" was revealed, barnacle-free, and ready for a steam… to Stellwagen Bank!

Gary Esper started diving in the late 80's, with lobsters off the Cape Ann rocks the usual target. We would throw some beers in the cooler, pack up the van with scuba tanks and fishing gear. Mike Moynahan and another lifelong friend, Brian Caulfield, would round out the dive squad. John Rice would jump in alongside me to help with the gear, and we'd point Gary's school-bus yellow, C20 Chevy van to Magnolia, Gloucester, or Rockport. Of course, once we got there, it took the guys some time to gear up. Meanwhile, John and I would cart some tanks down to the entry point off the rocks, with surf rods and a bag of plugs, and more often than not, we'd have hooked up with a couple of decent bass before the guys got down to us. John and I never really took to scuba, although maybe dabbled with a dive or two. Gary, on the other hand, went on to become a master diver.

Soon, the target of the dives evolved into something otherworldly. Lobsters and scallops were great, and we reaped the benefits; but Captain Esper had caught the bug of a different kind. Treasure! Not long after, trips to salvage copper spikes from the wreck of the USS New Hampshire, an 1800s warship that had sunk off Manchester-By-The-Sea. But, these weren't just any old spikes. They carried the stamp of Paul Revere's foundry. Yes, *the* Paul Revere. We even managed to sell a few for a pretty penny. Treasure fever had him in her grips, and some years later, the timing was right, and Gary had the ear of a few people willing to take a chance on an investment.

The Margaret was a fully-rigged tall ship, built in Boston in the late 1700's, launching in 1791. She carried eight cannon, and swivel guns, and was primarily used for maritime trade. Marking many voyages across the oceans, the Margaret was reportedly on a trip from Boston to Portsmouth when she was wrecked on Gooseberry Rocks off the Salem and Marblehead coast of Massachusetts, just south of Gloucester. Gary had recently worked a deal, crossed his T's, dotted his I's, and now held the claim with the State for the area for archeological salvage.

What treasures might lay beneath rubble was not totally clear. The manifest included a variety of what would be highly valued artifacts, and certainly there would be contraband, an estimated value expected well over a million dollars. In relatively shallow water, this made it even more attractive, and a seemingly worthy sell.

The first thing Gary did with his investor money was to secure a boat suitable for working offshore. The Sea Tek found a home in a slip at the Beverlyport Marina, where it was worked and outfitted, prepped and readied for the first season. In the spring of 2006, we were watching the paint dry, as they say, after we scrubbed, sanded, and applied the lipstick to the hull. A decent salary and strategy lured Mike and another old friend, diver Alex Bezkorovainy, to round out the crew, and Sea Tek Recovery was born.

The Summer of 2006 was an interesting time for me. It had been a few months since I moved out of what used to be my house. My ex-wife Gina and I had essentially separated late in early Autumn of 2005, and I had hip surgery that December. Basically, I was in a dark place for a few months while juggling the emotional and physical roller-coaster, but in March of 2006 I was feeling good. I found a sweet, big apartment, almost a whole house really, where my sixteen-year-old stepdaughter, Kasey, would feel comfortable. That was really the hardest part, tearing at my heartstrings, having to leave my *daughter*, who I helped raise for twelve years. But soon, I had settled into my own place, and the next few months were spent recovering, hitting the gym, and talking to the ladies in between trips to the marina to help Gary with the boat.

A girlfriend in upstate New York soon occupied every second weekend, but the others? Well, those weekends were spent topside on the Sea Tek, helping with dry-suits and scuba gear, scanning for ballast piles and artifacts, and eating fresh lobster and scallops just pulled from the bottom. Cold beer was the water for this salty group of pirates, cleansing our palettes and dreaming of riches ten miles from port. But other riches awaited offshore, and on off days, when the stars aligned, all roads led to Stellwagen.

It was mid-July 2006, and hot as hell. John and I walked down the ramp to the Sea Tek, now bobbing slightly at the slip. The sun was low in the sky, yet the summer days held off the darkness as Gary greeted us at the rail. He had a bucket of scallops they just scored off the deep water at Eagle Island, while taking a break from laying out a grid on a site they were working near Gooseberry Rocks. We casually cleaned them, tossing guts over the side to hungry schoolie stripers, and as soon as the sun set they were sizzling in a pan on a Coleman grill, with just a bit of butter, salt, and pepper. As simple as it gets, but the best damned scallops ever.

After dinner, we took stock of inventory. Eggs, bacon, coffee, water, beer, and ice. Check. We had the food and beverages covered, but more importantly, we needed to also attend to our fishing gear. This is where we fell short. We were still relative novices to the Bluefin Tuna scene. More importantly, we knew what we wanted to do, and had an idea how to go about doing it; but we were painfully under-gunned for the game. Our rod and reel setups basically consisted of a few striper trolling rods, and one heavy-duty spinning rod with a Fin-Nor reel to match. School-sized tuna was what we were hoping for, but we knew anything was possible.

We had sixty-to-eighty-pound leader material, heavy terminal tackle, a small spreader bar with green squid bulbs, a long-running, single Sluggo bait (soft plastic eel), and something that was new to the scene, Rapala X-Rap, deep-running swimming plugs. I had just read about these plugs, where southern skippers were crushing fish in thirty to forty feet of water down off Florida, so I had picked up a few in bonito and mackerel color to see if they could entice our northern fish. With the checklist covered, we hit the deck, literally, and rolled up in our blankets awaiting a two a.m. roll-call.

Ready or not, we were raising the black flag and heading for the bank. Arghhhh, me hearties! Our eyes were wet with a salty mist, as the channel markers glowed mysteriously through the calm blackness. The dew-covered blankets were stowed, engines roared awake, ropes were untied and coffee was brewed. The Sea Tek glided effortlessly on a flat sea, out past Misery and Baker's Islands, and the light from Gary's laptop shone eerily in the cabin. A course was set for the Northwest corner of Stellwagen Bank, an incredible marine sanctuary where whales play and tunas thrive, feeding on the baitfish confused by the upwelling when the current hits the wall of the bank, pushing waters from close to two hundred feet to as little as eighty.

We had our sights set on the tip of the bottom of the corner, where the plan was to follow the edge east and zigzag back along after a certain distance. The two-hour steam put us just off the edge after a steady ten knots from the heavy boat, its single screw creating what we hoped would be an enticing draw for hungry predators, mimicking frantic baitfish like herring and mackerel. A brilliant sunrise was now cresting, and the air felt heavy even with a slightly growing breeze.

We set the spreads with a top rod from above the cabin, running the sluggo way back where the wakes faded into blue. The starboard rigger ran the spreader bar, the squid bulbs sizzling on the surface. The port side outrigger had a bonito-colored X-Rap40 swimmer, and finally, pinned to the stern in close, another X-Rap40 in mackerel, just behind the boat. All was right in the world. The eggs and bacon had hit the plates. The coffee was still hot, and the lures were running like a machine. Now, all we had to do was sit back and wait. Or… so we thought. Bam! Fish on!

The port-side rigger running an X-Rap was crushed, line snapping from the clip and peeling from the reel on the trolling rod. Gary slowed the boat as John and I went to work. I cleared the other lines, John went to get cranking, but the fight was not what we initially expected after the big hit. The weight was there, but there was no searing run we were expecting from what we initially interpreted as a school tuna. It became quite clear what we were dealing with when a bloated striper appeared off the port-side rail, the Rapala plug clearly embedded in the corner of its jaw.

It was a true butterball of a bass, which had I caught off the beach would've left me feeling as high as a Snoop Dogg and Willie Nelson hyperbaric chamber. But, the Stellwagen waters fall within the EEZ, otherwise known as the U.S Exclusive Economic Zone, which begins three nautical miles of our east and west coasts, excluding the Gulf of Mexico. The problem is that these Federal waters are closed to Striped

Bass fishing. Tuna? Groundfish? Sure. Not stripers. By-catch of course happens, as does poaching, but by the rule of the sea, no bass can be harvested. What does this mean? Well, for one, it means you have a good chance of catching huge bass mixed in with your targeted species, and that day was our introduction to this side note.

Fish over fifty inches, ranging from thirty to fifty pounds, were destroying our swimming plugs. We had to have a sniff on the spreader bar or the long lined slug, but we also didn't have the tuna we were searching for... yet. It was late morning when we saw the whales ahead, rolling on the surface. The chart plotter showed a hump in eighty feet of water coming up. Then the X-Rap pinned off the stern went off.

The sixty-pound mono line was dumping off the old Penn trolling reel as Gary pulled the throttles back, and now the reel had slowed after taking half of it. I grabbed the rod, which was creaking and cracking under the strain of the beast below. An incredibly strong fish which I could do nothing with. It was complete chaos. Gary, John, humpbacks, blue skies, blue water, mackerel, a cauldron of sounds and sights, and me. I had brought a knife to a gunfight and was looking down the barrel of a .44 magnum. The most powerful handgun in the world. Did I feel lucky? This is when Dirty Harry would've chuckled.

Good times on the Sea Tek.

I had no idea how big the creature was. One hundred pounds? Two hundred? Bigger? It didn't matter. When I tightened up the star drag, the drag locked up, doubling the rod until the point of breaking. When I loosened the drag just a fraction, it was as if there were no drag pressure at all, the spool simply spinning wildly. We fought the fish for some time, or should I say, the fish fought us for some time, until I accepted that we would never see the fish. With that, I kept the drag locked and just held on until the rod exploded.

Frustrated, cursing myself for not being prepared, I pulled the rod from the holder, raised it to the heavens, and launched it through the air to find a home amongst the crabs. We had some work to do if we wanted a chance the next time out.

In what seemed like days, but was more likely a couple of weeks, the weather window and the schedule opened for us again, giving us our second shot at Stellwagen Bluefin. Regardless of how many days had passed, we hadn't wasted our time daydreaming of fish, but went about the task of gearing up for the next expedition. Gone were the striper rods, so laughably incapable of handling school tuna, other than football-sized specimens. Now in place were two 50W offshore reels, a two speed Penn international and a counterpart from Okuma. Both 50s were loaded with a backing of braided line, and hundreds of yards of 80lb mono. Add to that a Penn 30W, loaded with fifty-pound mono, and the heavy-duty Fin-Nor/Penn spinning outfit; and we definitely felt like we had more "gunpowder" in the kegs, or at least a fighting chance. Another early morning launch put us on the edge of the bank, with a repeat of the spread from our previous outing deployed.

Stellwagen was coated in a swirling pea-soup fog, with distant motors humming on the troll, except for one trust-fund boat that roared directly past our bow without hesitation. If that Gilligan made it back to port in one piece, it would be a miracle. Regardless, the fishing began as it did our last time out. The X-Rap was crushed, snapping off the rigger. Seconds later, the stern-pinned diving swimmer also went off. Again, not Bluefin, but twin, mid-thirty - pound Striped Bass. A healthy release for both fish, and we were back at it, with a steady pick of bass, including a couple over fifty inches. A Bluefish. Another bass. And the sun getting high.

UNTIL THE NEXT TIDE

It was now after noontime, and we decided to move up on the bank, targeting a hump in eighty feet of water. As we neared the target on the chart plotter, the surface of the water took on a flat, greasy appearance, almost as if someone had poured olive oil on a mirror. It was hot and hypnotizing, and then, as if a mirage had revealed itself, a slice of fin broke the mirror. I calmly called out the scene to Gary, and asked him to slowly cut the boat towards the fish, the lures getting drawn closer to the fading ripples of the mirage.

The 30W came to life as the tuna hammered the bonito-colored plug, and the fight was on. It wasn't a giant, but it was perfect. Our first tuna on the Sea Tek! Gary, John, and I took turns fighting the fish, if only to give each of us a share of the first Bluefin fought off the treasure salvage boat. Although any one of us could've easily handled the sixty-pound fish, we were a band of pirates, brothers of the sea, and long-time friends. Heinekens and Budweisers rattled in the cooler, and with the fish bled and wrapped in ice, we headed for the marina.

For those who may be unaware, Beverlyport Marina is just over the bridge from Salem, Massachusetts. Usually, this wouldn't play a part in any a salty dog's fishtales, and the proximity to the country's most famous supernatural village would typically end up as a side note, but not on this day. The 1690's may be well over three-hundred years in the past, but witches still wander the streets and the docks of the north shore. And, as fate would play out, one lived in a powerless hulk of a stationary sailboat taking up a slip on the other end of the dock.

She looked like a brunette version of Stevie Nicks, flowing dresses and scarves that could've passed for the wardrobe from the set of *Hocus Pocus*. Pretty in a twisted sort of way, with eyes that tried and failed to hide the crazy chick inside. Her name, if she ever gave one, would've been forgotten by the train wreck vision, so for the sake of her dockside baptism, let's call her Hagatha.

Hagatha was on a mission, as she floated down the dock toward the happy pirates, celebrating with cold beers, eyeing the tuna fish bathed in ice. We laid the fish out along the deck boards, and somewhat less than expertly began carving the flanks into steaks, destined for friends and family, backyards and barbecues. Pepper-crusted and seared. A little wasabi. The prize for finally pulling it together ourselves, a surfcaster's coronation, if you will.

But Hagatha had no concern for celebrations. No, she had something else occupying that part of her brain that seemed soaked in black magic, and had a question for us pirates. "Can I have an eyeball?" You know, most would say I'm never at a loss for words, but there it was. I looked at John and Gary and saw the same dumbfounded expression I'm sure was painted my face. "Uhhh… sure" was muttered in mutual agreement, and then the follow-up from Hagatha: "Can I have a fin, too?"

Okay, now the words started flowing. Laughing, out came "What the fuck do you want with these?" Without providing too much background, Hagatha revealed she had plans for her boss, who had apparently done something to bring out the inner wicked witch in her. Wishing her on her way, fish parts in hand, she faded into the coven

185

of her derelict sailboat. That would be the first and last time we saw Hagatha.

Our indoctrination into the Sacred Church of Stellwagen Bluefin had finally been realized. Now, we had a game plan that had produced results. The following weeks, well into the fall season that year, we managed multiple hookups. More big stripers, more big Bluefish, and more importantly, more tuna. No real giants hit the deck, but many fish in the one-hundred to one-hundred-sixty pound range took a liking to our Rapala X-Rap patterns and our trolling technique. We had it dialed in, where three rods were running the deep-diving plugs, and another either a spreader bar or a long distance sluggo on top. Soon, word began to spread throughout the area about the results we were getting with the Rapalas, and other recreational, so-called sharpies, took notice.

One day in particular, we were carting our gear down the dock to the boat slip, and passed a couple of guys who were gearing up themselves. A short greeting and discussion on what we were doing had these dudes raising eyebrows, questioning under their breath about our chances for success. Later that day, their skepticism was erased with a hint of envy on their part.

The three amigos, or stooges (take your pick) were back on the bank, this time, accompanied by a local kid, Dennis, who worked around the marina. It was good to have an extra hand on board (literally), as I had just had carpal tunnel syndrome a couple of weeks earlier, and had a brace on my left hand, but right off the bat, as soon as we got close to the edge of the bank, we knew we were in for a good day.

We had a spreader bar and two trolling outfits with deep divers, and it took my heavy spinning rod, snapped on a mackerel thirty-foot diver, and let it out far back in the wash, more so to tighten up my line and check the action on the lure. The X-Rap was slammed on the drop back as soon as I closed the bail. I don't if know if a passing school of fish saw it twitching on top before suddenly darting and diving forward, but it was hit seconds after I engaged the spool.

Big fish. Real big! The Bluefin screamed off the starboard side and Gary gunned the boat to keep pace. I was picking up some decent line, but as soon as we got in position to really crank up the fight, the fish took off again. We were chasing it down, gaining line, only to lose it again. Eventually, we had the fish closer to the boat, although we had still yet to see color. By this point, we had been switching off between deck hands, me in particular taking it easy to avoid any issues to my surgically repaired hand. Just when it looked as though we were about to step into the winner's circle, the hook pulled. Gone.

Initial disappointment was soon replaced with a determined effort to get right back at it. Now, cruising the edge towards the southeast, tracking our marks from previous hookups, the Penn 50W popped free of the downrigger and we were off to the races again. Another tough fish, but the rotation was set, and we took turns on the crank, until we saw a dark, purplish silver, beautiful Bluefin Tuna swim by the gunwale before pin-wheeling below in an exhausting effort. The gaff was on its mark, and moments later, a fish of one-hundred and sixty pounds was on the deck.

The regulations at that time allowed for two recreational fish, in a certain size-range, which this was within. We began prepping the fish by bleeding it and packing it in ice. I'll admit, we still didn't really know what we were doing, but we knew how to hook them, and that was half the fun. High fives followed, and we set out the spread to burn some more fuel, keeping an eye on the clock to try and get one more before melting ice sent us scurrying to the dock. For the hell of it, I had decided to throw the spinning reel into the trolling spread, especially after it had been hammered on the way out, and sure enough, it drew a strike. The spool of the Fin-Nor was practically smoking as fifty-pound braided line sizzled off the reel.

Again, the rotation was in play, but this time, we focused on the young guy. Dennis had never really caught anything big, mostly schoolie stripers, but he was putting the screws to this fish. Although not quite as big as the first fish, fighting on the spinning outfit made it a whole new game. Peering over the side, the silver sides reflected as the tuna made circles, until the one-hundred-ten-pound fish joined its fellow schoolmate on the deck.

Back at the slip, the *Twisted Teas* were going down easy when we spied the dudes from early morning. They were clearly ragged from a long day of nothing to show but raccoon eyes, but still we took the high road, refusing to say, "we told ya' so," although we yukked it up pretty good when they hit the gangplank to the parking lot. The tales of the Sea Tek would continue over the next couple of years—more fish, more laughs—before retiring to the boatyard, to be replaced by new boats, and new adventures still to come.

Chapter 18

The Wayfaring Angler – The Florida Keys, Silver Kings, and Other Things

Cape Cod, Cape Ann, Rhode Island, Maine. For decades, the local waters of the Northeast U.S.A have given me so many fish tales, with only a choice few included in these pages. But the dreams of unknown waters have always burned in the back of my mind. True-life accounts documented in books like "Tales of Fishing Virgin Seas" by the legendary novelist Zane Grey, and of course "The Old Man and the Sea" by Ernest Hemingway only added fuel to the smolder, turning to flame. While Hemingway's history would include an attraction to the same longitude and latitude, it would initially come to me by coincidence, a love that would grow to this day. The Florida Keys. Perhaps my favorite place in the world.

The funny thing is that my first venture to these fabled waters was more of an excuse to hang out with my older sister Erin and her girlfriend Eileen. In 2004, Erin and Eileen would become one of the nation's first same-sex married couples after legalization in Massachusetts, with Cape Cod as their home base. In the mid-80s they were living the good life in Fort Lauderdale. Life in the fast lane for two twentysomethings and an eighteen-year-old kid brother on the way. From twenty-five-cent daiquiri *happy hour* at the 15th Street Fisheries Bar and Grill, to concerts on Miami Beach, to last minute jaunts down Route One to Key West, it was one big party.

Then there was Eileen mooning us from the back of a homemade, wooden pickup truck while enroute to our next round of debauchery. A teenager's guide to South Florida would've read a whole lot different if I were to have written it back then. You know those experiences you try to hide from your hippocampus (yup, I went all geek-squad on you—that's where your memory lives), the memories you initially wish you could forget, but with time turn into cherished classics? That first trip to Key West qualifies.

Erin, Eileen, and I decided to go at the last minute. Four-hour drive. No worries, mon. And no packing an overnight bag, just hop in the car and hit the road. I had a t-shirt, flip-flops, underwear and the camo shorts I was wearing. The journey included a stop in Islamorada, where we took an impromptu dip to cool off. Back in the car, I stripped out of the shorts, wrapped myself in a towel, and rolled up my window with my shorts hanging out, drying in the breeze. Did I say it was hot? Damn, it's hot in Florida in the Summer. I think y'all know where this is going…

By the time I realized my shorts were gone, we had fewer miles ahead than behind us, so there was no turning back. The first thing we did when we got to Key West was to find me some pants. Erin jumped out and when she returned, I squeezed into one-size too-small, natural linen pants. "Uhh, this is going to be interesting." And it was, at least what I could remember later. You may have heard the saying, "a drinking town with a fishing problem?" Well, I'm guessing that was coined by a fellow who left the island in a fog, just as most do who partake in the Duval crawl. As in, Duval Street. Quite possibly the greatest stretch of good times, rum, and beach bums to grace the planet.

Sloppy Joe's, Capt. Tony's, Schooner Wharf, the list of bars goes on and on. And then there is the Garden of Eden, and the clothing optional rooftop called the Bull & Whistle. I've never made it to that top floor, which I'm guessing can be good and bad, but this first trip to Key West? Well, my too-tight linen pants didn't leave much to the imagination, and I did my best to stow the family jewels. We were a stone's throw away from the great treasure hunter, Mel Fisher's home port, where he had founded his treasure museum, featuring silver, gold, and precious gems from the salvaged wreck of the Spanish galleon the Atocha; but I was in no rush to add my emeralds to the collection. The Atocha's treasure would be enough to get this town a-singing; although, I'm pretty sure there was plenty of singing up and down Duval Street that night, after the sunset celebration capped off another day at Mallory Square.

Honestly, I'm pretty sure the rest of the evening was pushed out of my hippocampus by the all-to-common-in-Key-West Colombian blizzard. At the very least, my first Key West experience didn't disappoint, and it would be followed by many more, including one that could never be forgotten, featuring Fantasy Fest. A week-long party, ending in an all-out street party/parade on Halloween, where a would-be priest and his date—masquerading as a topless schoolgirl

Britney Spears—forced my hands on her breasts. Or anyone's hands that passed by. Naked beauties were painted like mermaids. Captain Morgan's boat sailed down Duval Street and the street flooded with rum. A true bacchanal experience if you're willing to risk your liver.

Key West might be the pot of gold at the end of the rainbow, as you jump from Key to Key, but you'll be missing out on the beauty of the true Keys if you fly into Key West. Key Largo, Marathon, Big Pine, and the funky little keys in between all have amazing things to see. Cool waterside bars, funky nature attractions, historic bridges, incredible beaches at Bahia Honda Key, maybe a *square grouper* if you're lucky, and incredible fishing. And then, you have perhaps my favorite Key, Islamorada.

Islamorada is actually a relatively short trip from Miami, approximately seventy-five miles from the airport, but it's really so much more. Transporting body and soul, it feels like the U.S. introduction to the Caribbean, when you start hopping the little islands of the mangrove-lined coral keys.

The water stretches out on your left and right, a crystal turquoise, with the central Route One your path to America's tropics. Of course, with that comes the beach-bum vibe, fishing shacks, and funky waterside bar and grills. Reggae and Buffett tunes fill the air. Margaritas flow freely, as you pass the welcome sign that proudly declares "WELCOME TO ISLAMORADA SPORT FISHING CAPITAL OF THE WORLD."

This isn't just tourism fluff either. The fishing culture is embedded in the fabric of this palm-lined village. The welcome mat for me was laid out on one of my early adventures with my sister, when Erin and Eileen introduced me to the "Miss Tradewinds," a deep-sea fishing party boat that specialized in bottom-fishing for whatever bites. That first trip was basically a sun-soaked sail, with snapper coming over the rails and cold beers coming out of the cooler. But from the marina to the dock, dock to the deck, I felt it. The draw to the laidback vibe, and southern breezes. Here, time moved by the tides, not by the ticking of a clock. I knew I'd be back.

Fast forward to the spring of 2005, which found me in an interesting place, physically and mentally. Physically, a childhood injury to my right hip was growing increasingly painful, soon to be addressed by a surgeon's knife. But mentally, the pain inside my head was ballooning as my marriage to my first wife, Gina, was fading into the history books. The writing was on the wall when she went on a "girl's trip" with one of her single friends. In reality, I think she was sick of being tied to a relationship. My stepdaughter Kasey was sixteen, and soon would be off to school. The classic mid-life-crisis was in motion; and by the time she returned, I could sense there was an end to this story. Of course, the emotions that come with any impending breakup were brewing. Anger, sadness, ebbs and flows. But, as with the tides, each one can bring a new surprise. Regardless, I needed an escape. and I knew just what place to go, where I could ease my worried mind.

In early May of that year, John Rice and I touched down in Miami with a plan to meet the *silver king*, aka the Tarpon. After sweet-talking the pretty girl (yes, I was already working on my game, figuring I'd soon be diving back into the *Singles* pool) at the Enterprise Car Rental desk, we soon found ourselves with an upgrade, heading south in a convertible in place of a run-of-the-mill coupe. Next stop… Lorelai's.

The Silver King of the Florida Keys

The brilliant blues of the Keys splayed out on either side as far as the eye could see, as we cruised US1, leaving Miami International Airport, passing through Homestead, Florida, where a 1992 hurricane still leaves a haunting impression. Key Largo introduces itself with a hint of the funky, Florida Keys vibe, which soon reveals itself through the mangrove-lined highway surrounded by the seas. To the East, the Atlantic, with a slight chop. To the West, the calmer waters of the Gulf of Mexico. It is this confluence that makes the Keys one of the world's most fertile fishing grounds. Options abound! Shortly after Tavernier Key, the *Sportfishing Capitol of the World* greets us, and Islamorada reveals itself in all its laid-back glory, as we make a right-turn at mile marker 82.

Lorelai's Bar and Grill couldn't be more perfect for the fishing crowd, sprinkled with mermaids, pirates, and reggae. John and I admired the Tarpon and Bonefish mounts displayed outside the path leading to the bar, just as Jimmy Buffet tunes greeted us, played by a salty dog on the small, sandy stage behind the outdoor grill. The guitarist in me wanted to join him and pick away at a few pirate songs; but the weary, thirsty traveler wanted a pina colada and a basket of fried grouper fingers. John and I settled in for lunch, boat drinks, and bronzed-skinned waitresses in Daisy Dukes. Ahh, yes, just what the doctor ordered, to wash away my troubled thoughts.

The morning greeted us with a forecast of the low nineties for the next three days. Sunshine, puffy Caribbean clouds, warm breeze, repeat. We coasted out of the somewhat inexpensive, no-frills hotel we were staying in (perfect for a couple of fishing fools), hit the bait shop, and decided to check out the underpasses of the many bridges that dot Route One. It took us maybe thirty minutes to go through the bucket of live shrimp we had; small jacks, snappers, and grunts the main recipients.

The rest of the morning, we bounced around, throwing small lures, and capped it off with a trip to Robbie's Marina to feed the Tarpon, a must-stop for those who've never experienced it. Also, a cool little seaside grill, but let's face it, almost everything is seaside in the Keys. We had a Tarpon charter scheduled for late day/early evening, and with more than a few hours to burn, John suggested an exotic way to pass the time.

It would be easy to miss Woody's if it wasn't for the name, and the signage declaring its entertainment offerings. It doesn't have a seaside view, but what is does have is something that may interest a couple of dudes, one who has longed for a girlfriend for a while, the other whose girl is turning into a memory. To just call it a strip club is easy enough, and really, that's all it is. But it's not hidden away like so many others. No, this is right on the main road. A proud establishment that doesn't hide what it is. Naked chicks? Sure. It was also a place where locals stop in for pizza and wings. And, music. Back in the day, the highlight, and I shit you not, was a band called "Big Dick and the Extenders." and from what I heard, Big Dick could really shred on the guitar. The reality of it all? John and I were there for tits and beer. The real surprise was, even though we got there around mid-afternoon, we spent a good amount of time drinking

197

beers, talking with the two girls working there, until it dawned on us, not one dancer had yet to hit the floor. I asked our waitress, "Candy," what gives, and she politely, in a southern belle kind of way, informed us that they didn't open until four p.m.. I guess a couple of northeast anglers were okay to lounge at the bar, as we were the only customers in the saloon.

A short time later, I looked up to see Candy walk on the dance floor, minus her Daisy Dukes and the rest of her clothing (except a garter), and she proceeded to pay close attention to us Yankee boys. For those who don't know, as is customary in these gentlemen's clubs, tips are very appreciated for the hard work the girls put in. Candy was getting up close and personal when I asked where I should put the dollar in my hand. "I've got three places you can put it," was her quick response. Tempting to say the least, especially in my mental condition. The dollar, of course, went in the garter. John and I finished our *lunchbreak*. It was Tarpon time!

Bud and Mary's marina is almost as legendary a part of Islamorada as the fishing, and has been a mainstay in the Florida Keys fishing community since 1944. When it was time to look at Tarpon charters, I knew this was the place. I had called to inquire some weeks prior, knowing that early May would be the beginning of the giant Tarpon migration in the upper Keys, and the good folks at B n' M's got us lined up with Captain David Applegate. John and I milled about dockside, waiting on the man lovingly referred to as Captain Apple. Out comes strolling a scruffy, mild-mannered gent with long white hair, looking like he could be a stand-in for David Crosby if they ever make a movie about Crosby, Stills, Nash, and Young.

We exchanged pleasantries, grabbed a bucket of crabs for bait, and walked the dock to Captain Apple's boat, a sixteen-foot skiff better suited for pulling crab pots than tangling with Tarpon. We skirted the gulf-side, bypassing one bridge for another until we settled on one channel bridge. I don't recall which channel, as the skippers have their favorites, including the bridges at channel two and channel five. Either way, Apple had high hopes that the big fish would finally show, as the real giants had yet to fill in with the local schools.

He had just begun to settle in place, hoping to catch the last of the tide and into the start of the next tide, when he cursed himself for forgetting his readers. With that, he pulled off his push pole, leaving it in place where we were anchoring for the tide, and blasted his way back to the dock. At the dock, Apple jumped ashore and high-tailed it to his truck to retrieve his glasses. At this point, John and I were basically saying "What the fuck… did we make a mistake… should we jump ship?" But no sooner had we questioned our guide than he returned, and we were hightailing it back to our spot at the channel. It would prove to be a very smart decision.

When we returned to our spot, the tide had started to dump from the gulf thru the bridges, toward the Atlantic side. Apple reset our anchoring spot, setting us up with two baitcasting outfits, drifting crabs under big corks back in the current toward the bridge. The tide was slowly cranking up, and we were battling with weeds fouling our bait, when I commented "there's a lot of grass flowing though," to which Apple replied, "That's not grass… this is grass!" and he pulled out a bag of weed.

John and I looked at each other. Well, I thought, if we don't catch any fish, at least we'll be happy. Apple packed his pipe and we passed around the sweet-smelling ganja, which proved to be the mojo we were waiting on. John's rod doubled over. Some fifty yards in the distance, a massive Tarpon estimated by Apple at one-hundred-twenty pounds, cleared the water. We threw off the anchor and gave chase. The silver king on the end of John's line jumped a half dozen times before we got close, as the Tarpon neared the bridge, seeking freedom that it presumed was on the Atlantic side. Before it could dart under the bridge, it decided to make things interesting by making a U-turn, wrapping around a crab pot.

Apple booked it over to the pot, where I was able to free the line. The fight was back on, at least for now. Thirty minutes into the fight, John was giving it all he had. I stepped on the forward deck, angling for a good picture of the Tarpon in one of its signature jumps. And then, the fish jumped… and was gone. Just feet from the boat, leader on the reel, technically as Tarpon fishermen refer to as a "caught fish." But we never got a hand on it. I was up next.

Back at our spot, all thoughts of weed, grass, pot or crab pots, or anything other than Tarpon quickly evaporated. I wanted to experience the incredible battle I just witnessed for myself. I didn't have to wait long. As I was letting my crab float back, it neared the bridge as did the previous drift, and was crushed. A massive silver king took flight, this time quickly charging under the bridge overpass.

Apple fired up the motor and we raced to follow the giant fish. We watched as the fish jumped in what seemed at least one hundred yards out. Its mirrored sides reflected the sun, now low in the sky to our west, lighting up the white water as the splash gave way. Strong fish. Big fish. I'd never felt a power like this from an animal on the other end of the line. All I could do was hold on, and try to gain line when I could.

The Tarpon had a change of mind, and headed back under the bridge. The skipper deftly navigated us in chase, having to go around one piling, then diagonally through another, until we were clear on the gulf-side once again. But not clear for long. The speed of the fish had it circle us, wrapping the line under the lower unit of the outboard motor. Incredibly, the forty pound line avoided the prop, as Apple turned the boat, killed the motor, raised the prop, and freed the line. We were still tight!

The back and forth continued, and the silver king once again decided the Atlantic was where it wanted to be. Back under the bridge again, we followed in hot pursuit. I had been doing everything possible to keep the rod tip low, so as not to allow the Tarpon to gulp air. An uncommon trait of the Tarpon is that it not only breathes oxygen from the water, but also by gulping air, allowing it to swim in brackish, low-oxygenated waters. But this is also something it can do to restore energy, much like Popeye eating spinach. And this fish was strong to the finish!

The sun was gone now, darkness enveloped us. The sound of Tarpon could be heard slurping bait everywhere. Left, right, all around us. Sharks would surely be nearby. I needed to boat this fish or break it off before it fell to a sharp-toothed Bull Shark, and I surely didn't want to break it off. I could barely speak, drenched in sweat. John asked me what he could do. "Water!" was all I could say. One hour and twenty minutes in, I had my Tarpon boatside. A one-hundred-and-forty-pound behemoth. A valiant warrior who was so close to winning the battle, but one who would gain his freedom, and live to swim another day. My first Tarpon trip, my first Tarpon, and I had David Crosby's lookalike and his medicine bag to thank for it.

Back at the dock, John and I thanked Captain Apple, and he wished us well, sending us off with a parting gift, a pinch from his medicine bag. The following day, we had a morning charter offshore to the Islamorada humps, doing battle with some feisty but small blackfin tuna. It was a day that would've been memorable on its own, if not for the incredible day before. Nevertheless, we enjoyed some of our catch back at the dockside bar, seared with black peppercorn, and capped off the day with a cold drink or two at Lorelai's, where we were pleased to see Apple and his lady doing the same. That was the last I would see of Captain David Applegate, and my last inquiry as to his whereabouts told tale of his moving on to parts south of Bud n' Mary's.

In the years since my first Tarpon, I've returned many times to Islamorada, fishing with a guide named Gunner Guthrie. A great deal younger than Apple, but a fine fisherman and guide all on his own, Gunner has since hooked me up with many a Tarpon, and putting these words to paper has me yearning for a return trip to the channel bridges of Islamorada.

Chapter 19

The Wayfaring Angler – Costa Rica, Pura Vida

There's a reason Steven Spielberg picked Costa Rica as the location to film his legendary movie *Jurassic Park*. With its sprawling coastline and vast stretches of unspoiled wilderness comprised of jungles and rainforests, it *feels* pre-historic. Inland, you'll find rolling hills where cowboys work the fields, and cattle, a surprise for the first-time tourist. Here, a vibe permeates the soul of the land and sea from coast to coast, where Ticos and Ticas (the Costa Rican term for local men and women), expats, eco-tourists, fishermen, and farmers all live the "Pura Vida" lifestyle. Pure life. A simple life, welcoming to locals and foreigners alike.

It was this lifestyle, combined with a wandering spirit, that first drew my sister Erin and her wife Eileen to go on an adventure to this amazing country in the heart of Central America. Soon thereafter, they would regale us with tales of incredible wildlife, the warmth of the Ticos and Ticas, and the wonders that this beautiful country had to offer. In the early 2000s, Costa Rica had yet to grow into an "it" destination, and other than expatriates, tourism was just beginning to take off. Sure, adventurous travelers would seek out what was then considered a remote destination, well before Costa Rica would appear as a prize-package on Wheel of Fortune. But even George Bailey would've had a travel poster for Costa Rica tucked under his arm if he knew *what a wonderful life* existed there. Hee haw!

Outside the main urban areas, like the capitol city of San Jose, Costa Rica is rugged and remote in parts, even dangerous. There are snakes, jaguars, and infinite numbers of insects—the place is alive, a vibrant land made for exploration, with seas made for adventure. Once upon a time, it was a mysterious destination to many, but thanks to cold New England winters and the Sunday morning fishing shows that I loved, I knew very much what Costa Rica had to offer a fisherman.

My favorite show, produced and hosted by the late, great Jose Wejebe, was *Spanish Fly*. Jose was a Cuban-born angler, producer, director, and musician, and was a fixture in the Florida Keys. His positive and easy-going attitude made him completely likable, and someone I truly admired. Unfortunately, Jose perished on April 6th, 2012, when he crashed his solo-piloted aircraft in the everglades. But it was Jose, and his TV compadres, who introduced me to the fishing opportunities that existed in Costa Rican waters. Wild waters, teeming with exotic fish, the type of creatures Zane Grey would recall in his famous writings. In April of 2002, thanks to a family trip, I would get a chance to fish the waters I had only dreamed of.

The *Swiss Family Robinson* touched down in San Jose after a six hour journey from Boston. Our group consisted of Erin, Eileen, their son Jake, my former wife Gina, daughter Kasey, and myself, along with a couple of E&E's friends. After a long day, the first night was spent in a nearby hotel, in preparation for a cross-country trek the next morning. We rented a couple of Toyota Land Cruisers, the funky, jungle-exploring kind you typically only see on the Discovery channel. The following morning, our adventure took off, as we headed west toward the Pacific.

Our destination on the first part of the trip was the Cloud Forest Biological Preserve in Monteverde, an amazing and temperate area filled with extraordinary wildlife, including quetzals, a Central American bird with incredible colors and super-long tail feathers. They are a rare sight, but one which is very possible in the cloud forest region.

Before we could enjoy Monteverde, we had to contend with the drive. We took turns navigating the three-to-four-hour trip, which took us along very narrow roads, running the sides of incredibly steep mountains. Definitely not for the anxious driver! Passing through small villages, there were also rutted roads, native folks on dirt bikes, and local police to deal with. It's recommended to keep a few US dollars at hand to contend with officers who want to make trouble for those they catch "speeding." Luckily we kept to the law of the land and didn't even see any police outside of the city.

There were pit stops along the way to take pictures of white-faced capuchin and spider monkeys, bouncing about here and there. Then there were the modern day Jurassic encounters. Some of the bridges we crossed had posted warning signs, and one we stopped at, passing over a muddy creek below, revealed the live-action reason why. A few people were at the railing, perhaps a mere twenty feet above the creek, tossing raw chicken to the crocodiles below. Uh… note to self. No cooling off by jumping off bridges in Costa Rica!

After checking into our beautiful jungle hotel, we headed over to the Preserve where we met a guide who took us on a hike through the cloud forest, where we indeed spotted the elusive Quetzal. Other jungle creatures appeared to take notice, as toucans and other amazing birds took to the skies. Howler monkeys gave the occasional growl, voicing their approval or disapproval. Hard to tell when they sound like a monster living in the trees. The capper of our trip to the area was a zip-line through the canopy of the cloud forest, over a five-hundred-foot ravine. If you want to get up close and personal with the treetop dwellers, this is the way. We all climbed our way to the top of the jungle, harnessed up, and took flight. A totally amazing, once-in-a-lifetime adventure. Although, I'm not sure the two young guides working the landing pad felt the same way when this two-hundred-fifty-pound American came flying toward them. I saw a hint of fear in their eyes, but, I made sure to save them from becoming Jurassic Park's latest victim. Our first stop was concluded. Now, we were off to the volcano!

The Arenal Volcano stands watching over the town of LaFortuna and Lake Arenal, and can only be described as majestic. Yes, I know, what a cliché of a term, but it's true. Arenal is massive at over 5400 feet tall, with a perfect cone-top. This is one volcano that lives up to the imaginations of generations of children and millions of boxes of crayons used to draw dinosaurs under the shadow of an erupting mount. A true movie poster volcano, it regularly spews lava down its slopes and puffs swirling plumes skyward.

The last major eruption was in 1968, burying three villages, and it remained active until 2010, when the great mountain went into a state of rest. Although still alive, its eruptions have ceased for now. Back in 2002, it was very much still flexing its might. Luckily for us, the night sky was clear as the sun left for the day, the volcano's lava fields beautifully painting its sides. You really don't know until you see it, the power of nature. The heart of the earth showing itself. You can stare at it endlessly, and it felt as if we were.

After another long trek, we found ourselves at the beautiful Tabacon Thermal Resort on a cliffside with a clear view of the beast of a volcano. After breaking ourselves away from the hypnotizing view, the resort pool welcomed us, and the swim-up pool bar provided the refreshment. And one amazing perk. Feeding the pool are two mountain creeks that converge into one. One, steaming hot, is heated by underground volcanic springs. The other, icy-cold mountain water. The creeks meet in natural formations, adorned with incredible, human touches, the perfect spot for a tropical beverage. You can almost sense the healing powers. Our would-be spiritual retreat with margaritas would come to an end the following morning, when we departed for stop number three, and the ocean beckoned. I would finally make it to the Pacific!

The journey from Arenal took us through green, rolling hills, farmland dotted with cattle, dusty villages, and finally to the tropical shores of Puntarenas, on the Gulf of Nicoya. From there, we boarded a ferry bound for the small, expat town of Montezuma. Montezuma was a small beach village, but with just enough bars, restaurants, and nice hotels to make any traveler feel comfortable. The chill, Pura Vida vibe filled every corner of this Pacific outpost on the Nicoya Peninsula, near the southwestern tip of Cabo Blanco, and here is where my Central American angling adventure really began.

Erin and Eileen had the pleasure of visiting the area previously, becoming good friends with one of the local Ticos, Gerardo, and his amigos. Thanks to them, we were in good shape to quickly acquaint ourselves with the town. Our main stay was in the beautiful Sano Banano Beachside hotel, which included a couple of nights sleeping in beachside cabanas. The primary hotel had the usual amenities—bar, pool, air conditioning—but the cabanas? They were bare bones, and you wouldn't want it any other way. Literally on the beach, under the edge of the swaying palms. No air conditioning, which when first getting into town would seemingly have one turning around and heading for Alaska. The proximity to the equator, combined with ultra-humidity, combined into sauna like conditions. But beachside? Amazingly, the cabanas with open windows and doors, welcomed cooling breezes all through the day and night, with a ceiling fan adding to one's comfort. It was actually quite pleasant.

Our group rotated staying in the cabanas, with one couple staying for two nights, while the others watched the kids at the hotel rooms. We were surprised to find that a walk along the beach was required to reach the cabana. While hotel staff took our bags in an oversand buggy, we walked beside the ocean. A large silver fish flashed though the clear blue waves as we strolled the beach, and the experience added magic to our adventure. Later that night, that image played in my head as the rolling surf lulled me to sleep.

The following morning, while the rest of our traveling show saddled up on horseback to reach a remote waterfall down the coast, I was busy going over my tackle for a surfcasting jaunt down the same coastline. My sights were set on Roosterfish, a species long on my bucket list, along with whatever other tropical species might find my offerings tempting. My weapon was a ten-foot surf rod, with lures and plugs I would typically be tossing around Cape Cod for big stripers and blues, two-ounce pencil poppers, swimming plugs, and metal jigs.

The morning air was already steamy, though bearable, but the rays of the sun? I could feel its intensity on every inch of exposed skin. Shorts, a long-sleeved t-shirt, a hat, and ample sunblock were a necessity. The walk down the shoreline took me on and off the beach, climbing rugged, volcanic rocks up into the jungle, and then back to the sand. An island down the shore—just past an outcropping of the very same volcanic rocks—looked like a good place to take a few casts.

I began a series of fan casts, plying the waters for any hungry fish, and soon I found myself having waded in almost chest deep over a smooth, clear, sandy bottom. Picture perfect. It was then that I looked to my left and then to my right, realizing I was far from the cabanas, with not another soul in sight. My horseback-riding companions had long since faded down the beach, and I was left in seclusion. The little fisherman in the back of my mind sent my thoughts to a wary place.

If some harm should come my way, what would become of me? Typically, I'd shrug this off as foolish paranoia, but not this time. I'll be the first to admit, I'm not scared of sharks. In fact, I love sharks… but should something unfortunate happen to me, I was in a totally remote spot, where no one knew to look for me. That was enough to get me out of the water, at least to the shallows of the surfline.

Just down the beach to my left, a small creek poured into the sea, and I decided to investigate. As I neared, I could see it had cut a deep bank along some rocks leading into the ocean, maybe three to four feet in depth. A few large shadows stayed inside the shadow-line along the rocks. I cautiously approached, keeping low so as not to spook the fish, and tossed a five-inch Crystal Minnow swimming plug just up the creek, and snapped the rod tip as it neared the shadows. In a frantic take, the water exploded as a fish grabbed the plug, bolting to open water. After a determined back and forth, I swam a beautiful three-foot Pacific Snook onto the sand.

After patting myself on the back (no cell phone camera for me back then), I quickly got the fish back in the water and sneakily made my way back over to the creek. The shadows had regrouped and another cast amazingly resulted in another hookup. Not quite as large, but still a nice snook that proceeded to froth the water as it took to the air, throwing the hooks back at me. I would have to wait quite a few more minutes for the fish to calm down and return to their stage, with many a cast ignored, until finally one couldn't resist, and I was tight again. This time, I would stay tight, and another nice snook of thirty-four inches would follow in a healthy release. By now, the sun was getting higher, and my comfort level convinced me to fish my way back toward home base.

The volcanic outcropping I had passed on my down the beach stretched out, beckoning me to cast from its rugged point. It was truly a fascinating patch of coast: a hard, alien-like surface, with thousands of small holes dotting it. Every step sent the little red crabs who inhabited these holes scurrying for safety, sinking within, only to emerge when my footsteps faded. At the edge of the furthest point, there was an approximate three-foot drop to the water's surface. I couldn't see bottom, and never bothered to check the actual depth by dropping a jig, but it was surely deep. I could see the water change color along the way out, the bottom fading to deep, purple-blue darkness, but with a clarity that was undeniable. The slight swell crashed along the ledge, throwing a bit of spray into the air, a much-welcomed relief from the midday cauldron of the sun. It looked and felt like the home of Roosterfish.

For those of you unfamiliar, Roosterfish get their name from the large, comb-like dorsal fins atop their back. A formidable gamefish, battling with the power like a giant jackfish, capable of reaching one-hundred pounds, although a fifty-pounder is considered a real trophy catch. Like I said, a bucket list fish for me. A swift lure change from the swimmer to a Gibbs two-and-a-half-ounce, mackerel-colored pencil popper, and I was ready. With a couple of nice snook under my belt, my day was already an overwhelming success, so I had no expectations. The possibility of catching a Roosterfish still seemed like a striper fisherman's dream, but that would soon change. Ten minutes into casting, other than occasional baitfish skirting the ledges, I had not seen any other signs of life.

Suddenly, behind my dancing pencil popper, there appeared the tips of a black, comb-like dorsal fin. As if it were a mirage, I watched as the pursuit increased, the Roosterfish zigging ang zagging, dorsals fully exposed now, taking a broad swipe, and missing the plug, and immediately turning back for a savage strike. My rod buckled, bent hard, and in an instant, my line was peeling from my spinning reel, as what I estimated to be a thirty-five to forty pound rooster made a sizzling run. The fight continued, give and take soon became more take, and I worked the big fish closer. Now was the time to seek a landing spot. I looked over the rocky terrain, saw a spot slightly lower to the water, and made a decision to try and lay down upon the edge to hopefully grab the fish by its massive tail. I had won! I had checked a dream fish off the bucket list! All I had to do was navigate the edge, hold my rod high, and work the fish to me… plink!

No! Impossible! As I crouched down to make my move, the rooster made one last ditch effort, and popped the hook from its mouth. Devastated. Broken-hearted. There are plenty of words to describe what I was feeling, but only an angler really knows the feeling of losing a big fish. This one hurt a little more than that. I've lost big stripers and tuna before. It happens to all of us who ply the waters, but this one? In this place? It would take some time before the haunting faded into a special memory of an opportunity and great battle with a magical fish. One to treasure until I get a second chance to fulfill this bucket list entry.

Not to let my mental state send me off the rocks just yet, I took a few deep breaths, righted my mind, and settled in for a few more casts before calling it quits. Sadly, there would be no consolation prize on this day, though a few casts later, I was treated to the sight of a large Cubera Snapper slowly rising under my plug, only to sink back to the depths. That, and the realization that I had neglected to reapply sunblock to the backs of my hands (now a frightening purple), sent me headed back to home base, where I hoped tequila would ease the sting of not only sunburn, but of dreams lost.

Chapter 20

The Wayfaring Angler – Costa Rica, Captain Hook, and the Pyrates

The following day, I hoped to erase the heartbreak of losing yesterday's rooster by hopping on a panga and trolling the waters off Cabo Blanco. The town beach of Montezuma has a small flotilla of small fishing boats called pangas on the sand, ready to launch for half day or full day fishing and snorkeling expeditions. These are usually charters set up straight from the crusty salts lounging beachside, and comprised of Ticos, expats, and vagabonds. That morning, I reached out to my sister's friend, Gerardo, and he set up with a salt-washed, shaggy blonde-haired and half-dreadlocked castaway, whose name I've long forgotten. An interesting dude at the first introduction, he appeared to be of German nationality, but spoke fluent Spanish and English. While young, he gave off the vibe of someone who left home a long time ago, and didn't want to be found.

After exchanging island pleasantries, we headed to his panga stowed up on the beach, loaded it with a few rods and a small cooler, and pushed the boat into the mostly gentle surf. I had now committed myself to the idea that this was my first real chance at hooking a billfish, whether sailfish or marlin. While just twenty-two feet, give or take, the boat looked capable of running two side rigs, and one straight back. We would be fishing in waters that saw little pressure from bigger sportfishing outfits, which should've given reason for optimism. The German hippie (although I might add, I was looking pretty much a hippie myself at the time) and I were just about to push off when he waved to someone on the beach to join us. Jogging toward us was a blonde, short-haired Chiquita worthy of a Sports Illustrated cover and sporting a tiny, white, barely-there bikini. I was paying for the character but I wasn't about to complain about this stowaway. Little did I know, it was going to be a quite interesting trip, but not for the reasons that now laid out across the front bench of the panga.

While the skipper skirted the coast toward the southeast tip of the Cape, his girlfriend—whom we'll call Elsa—worked on her tan. I kept a steady eye on the short trolling outfits, occasionally darting my gaze to the long running bait, far back in the middle of the spread. I had already released a couple of bonito, and my adrenalin was kicking up as we were seeing some action. Frigate birds skimmed the waters ahead. indicating there might be bigger fish nearby.

The deep rod popped; this time a small tuna was the prize. Onward we trolled, and the starboard side rigger popped the line; we were tight again. Another Yellowfin, slightly bigger, but still small for what we were after, hit the swimming plug. Elsa was oblivious to the action occurring to the rear of the boat, that is, oblivious until she heard the high-pitched screaming. The captain had just leadered the tuna, and was now holding the leader in the boat with the fish quivering and dangling at the end of the line when the tension gave way. The big swimming plug popped free of the fish's mouth, under extreme pressure, and one of the rear treble hooks buried itself deep in the man's thigh. That was the moment that this castaway captain inherited his new nickname—*Captain Hook*!

Chaos erupted on the boat as I cleared the lines. Captain Hook's scream had faded, to be replaced with his girlfriend's own cries until he acknowledged he was okay. The anxiety in the air had begun to subside as I talked with the captain, calming him down, and trying to convince him to immediately cut the trip short and head for the beach. Much to my amazement, he insisted on continuing with the charter to give me my money's worth. At this point, I thought he was slightly off his rocker; but he said "no, let's keep going." He just needed to do something about his leg. The big lure was dangling from the one treble hook, embedded into his flesh well past the barb. We had already clipped the line from the lure, but what of the lure itself?

At this point, Captain Hook was rambling in a mix of German, English, and Spanish, and Elsa was responding in *I don't know what*, when he got on the radio and started communicating with someone in Spanish. Spinning the boat about, we headed towards the tip of the Cape, and then around it heading north. In the distance, I could see a rather large fishing troller. As we got closer, the picture became clearer, but somehow, at the same time, surreal.

Ahead of us was an illegal fishing boat out of Nicaragua, forbidden from fishing these waters. On deck was a group of pirates, some armed with machine guns, and looking at us through suspicious eyes. We edged closer to the boat, near enough for Captain Hook to communicate with the pirates. Another figure appeared, carrying a heavy set of bolt cutters. Captain Hook was able to retrieve it mid-air as it was tossed from the pirate ship to our panga, and quickly dispatched the heavy split-ring on the lure connecting the hook to the plug. Now, left with just the hook hanging from flesh, he wrapped the leg in a t-shirt, and tossed the bolt cutters back to the mystery ship. A quick thank you, and a sigh of relief sent us on our way back towards the Cape.

I confirmed with Captain Hook regarding his intentions, assuring him that I was good to head back now; but again, he said no. Let's carry on. At this point, I resigned myself to take advantage of where we were at that point in time. We were here to fish, so… let's fish! Back out went the trolling rigs. Penn 30W international reels were back in action, slotted into the side riggers, which were bolted directly to the rail of the boat on each side.

We had gone maybe a hundred yards, just off the ledges of Cabo Blanco, deep water, lures alive and dancing, when the port side rig was slammed by a huge fish, followed by a stomach-churning screech of metal. This was again followed by a scream from the bellows of Captain Hook, but not one of pain. No, this was a howl of shock. The large fish that hit the port-side rigger had ripped the works from the side of the boat. Rod, reel, rigger. Gone. A hook hanging from his leg couldn't get him to head back in, but watching as hundreds of dollars in gear was ripped into the depths was all he could take. I had to contain the laughter bubbling inside me as I absorbed the insanity that had taken place over the last couple of hours, unsure whether Captain Hook could wash this bad mojo from the gunwales. Elsa remained silent, perhaps unsure of the superstitions of Captain Hook.

Back at the beach, I refrained from saying "I told you so," in regard to heading in after the hook-in-leg incident. Instead, I passed along a tip worthy of someone who needed a pick-me-up, and faded off the beach, never expecting to see Captain Hook and his mermaid again. Gina and Kasey met me at the little beachside grill, where I retold the story of Captain Hook and the pirates over a rum punch. Gina said the next day we would be snorkeling down the coast at a beautiful tropical island with our nephew Jake, and that would help erase any lingering bad mojo. It sounded like way to exorcise the demons from Cabo Blanco.

The next morning, I awoke with a renewed spring in my step, gathered our gear for the day, and headed for the pangas. The four of us were all smiles, anxious for an exciting day, swimming with amazing creatures in crystal clear water—the perfect recipe to wash away the previous day's tumultuous expedition. Kicking off our flip-flops, we barefooted it over the sand and were met with... Captain Hook???

Yes. Apparently, my misfortunate skipper of the previous day had put his injuries to both body and psyche behind him, and was now preparing to take us snorkeling. I don't know if he didn't want to be reminded of the prior day's outing, or buried it someplace deep inside, but we never spoke of it. Me, on the other hand? I was doing everything to keep it from taking me down, keeping focus on diving instead, to explore the reefs that surrounded us.

Surprisingly, the ride south was relatively smooth, with the wind at our backs, and the smile I had been faking soon became real. It was a beautiful day, and the shit that had gone down yesterday was history. The snorkeling was incredible. The location, amazing. We were all smiles. The day was capped with a beachside lunch, with cold cervezas for the adults, and Coca-Cola for the kids, which helped wash down the shore lunch of grilled chicken, jasmine rice, carrots, and cool ginger sauce. A perfect outing, or so I thought. We still had the trip back; but what could ruin a day like this?

Gina, Kasey, and Jake sat in the back of the panga, and I drew the short straw, sitting just in front of Captain Hook's console up front. With the wind no longer at our backs, and the tide change, we were now running into a steady chop, and it was doing a number on my back. By the time our beach was in sight, every wave was causing me to wince. As we got closer, I knew relief was near and I would soon be out of this cursed vessel. But Captain Hook had one last, parting gift for me.

I helped the others out of the boat, stepped on the rail, and jumped over the side. Little did know, the anchor rope had wrapped around my foot, coming tight as I jumped, and sending me head-down into the wash. A perfect faceplant in the sand. To this day, reminiscing about it is all the fuel needed for a laugh from my daughter Kasey, and my nephew Jake; but if my graceful exit can spark a chuckle, that's good enough for me. It was a fitting end to my time with Captain Hook.

The turn of the century welcomed tail-walking, Costa Rican Sailfish for my nephew, Jake Golden, and myself

Chapter 21

The Wayfaring Angler – Costa Rica, Quepos and Tailwalkers

Our Costa Rican adventure would conclude with a trip to the Quepos area, about mid-way down the coast from Montezuma, toward the border with Panama. After the ferry ride back across the Gulf of Nicoya, we followed a coastal route that took us through funky surf villages like Playa Hermosa and Jaco. Little shacks and beach bars dotted the outskirts, with surf dudes looking like they had found their place on the big blue. The surfing vibe fades as you near Quepos, soon morphing into a more pointed, and significant fishing vibe. Known primarily as the gateway to the famous Manual Antonio National Park, Quepos is also well-regarded as one of the best fishing destinations in Costa Rica. But first up, Manuel Antonio.

After awaking to the sound of howler monkeys in the trees, café con leche and fresh fruit got the day started at our hillside bungalows. The park was a short drive to the south, and the parking lot was anything but Disney-like. This was stress-free, welcoming, but still with a tourist feel. There were local vendors selling handmade wares, souvenirs, trinkets, leather goods, and local items showing the amazing, tropical wildlife. Fish, reptiles, jungle animals.

The path into the park leads through a short, wooded trail, worn and weathered with steep, dirt sides to the left and right. We were told the dark holes, dug in and lining the dirt walls, were tarantula holes. Monkeys swung overhead, as I noticed a small crowd looking at one particular hole. Going in for a closer look, I saw a large python peering out. Moving even closer, until a ranger spoke calmly from behind me to me. "Senor, be veryyyy careful. They are veryyyy fast."

Well, those that know me know I don't typically heed authority. Even to this day, my lovely wife Shannon, tongue firmly in cheek, happily shares "the rules don't apply to him" when I do something that goes against better judgment. But alas, as the ancient knight, protector of the Holy Grail, announced to Indiana Jones, I had "chosen wisely," and slowly backed away from the python photo shoot, and carried on with our entourage. The rest of the day was filled with enjoying the beauty Manuel Antonio had to offer, swimming in the cove, and seeking out the amazing wildlife that calls the park home. The day was capped with dinner at a restaurant just across the street from the marina, catering to the sea-worn folks wrapping up a charter offshore. Just the right spot to get me pumped for the next day's outing, water-logged echoes of the day's catches ringing in my ears.

Many weeks prior to departing on our Costa Rican adventure, I began researching the skippers in the Quepos region, finally settling on Captain Bryce Blair. A British Columbian transplant, Captain Bryce had produced some serious results from what I could gather from the turn-of-the-century world wide web. The internet had been around for many years, but was very much in its infancy compared to today, when just about everything has a review to turn to. From what I could gather, Bryce looked like a skipper who could give me a chance at a billfish.

In the morning, Bryce would greet us at the dock with his son, whose name I can't recall, at his boat, the name of which name I also cannot recall. Regardless, it was an approximate thirty-five-foot sportfisher, solid, well-equipped with all the modern tackle and needs to set us up with a comfortable ride, while still being outfitted to deal with any fish. My sister Erin and nephew Jake rounded out the crew for this trip, which was a short steam to the bluewater.

The bite had been relatively slow as of late, but sailfish were still showing in decent numbers, with the occasional marlin. The skipper's nineteen-year-old son expertly prepped the trolling outfits with attention to detail like a surgeon at work, and sporting the darkest tan I think a Canadian has ever had. Making this young man's work even more impressive, he was just getting over dengue fever, courtesy of a Central American mosquito!

The plan was simply stated, harder to execute. When a billfish came up in the spread of trolling lures, our mate would tease him in closer to the boat, for the "bait and switch," at which point, I would toss a baitfish, a rigged ballyhoo. If all went according to plan, the fish switches pursuit, and inhales my bait. In what seemed like only minutes since we put the trolling spread out, I did just that.

A large Pacific Sailfish left a frothy pocket of whitewater in the spread, as it just ate my ballyhoo, and peeled off line, heading for the horizon. The sail waved its huge dorsal from a distance as the fish took to the air, putting on a mighty display as it tail-walked across the waves. Surprisingly, we would not make eye contact with the sailfish again until I fought it near to the boat; but it did not shy out again during the battle. Instead, it bore down, fighting like a bulldog, keeping its head down. This actually worked in my favor as the likelihood of the hook being thrown was much less without taking the fight above the waves.

Regardless, that didn't deter the great fish from using its blazing speed. Thirty-pound monofilament sliced through the seacaps, spraying a rainbow sheen to the air. Soon, the fish was close. Amazingly beautiful and lit up with electric purples and blues from its fins, dark bars on its copper flanks, and that incredible sail, powerful and glowing. Its bill is a weapon for survival of the sea, but the mate grabbed the bill and the fish was mine.

We hauled the one-hundred-twenty-pound sailfish aboard for a couple of quick photographs, followed by a resurrecting drag by the bill alongside for a life-giving release. I thanked the fish gods for the gift of checking another specimen off the bucket list, and back on the troll we went. Erin stood by as the sole member of our cheerleading squad, as Jake and I did battle with the sea creatures. Now, it was ten-year-old Jake's turn. This time, a big Mahi-Mahi charged the spread, avoiding the teasers and hitting one of the trolled ballyhoos. Green and yellow took to the air, putting on an acrobatic display.

Jake fought the fish like a champ, a Cape Cod kid showing these tropical fish how it's done! What would be dinner soon came over the rail, headed for the icebox. We were back at it in a snap, and it wasn't long before the captain was calling frantically from the flybridge above. A large Blue Marlin had risen in the spread, darting from one lure to the next. The mate tried to tease the fish toward a bait before the fish lost interest and disappeared for good. A short while later, I was tight to a thirty-pound mahi, which would eventually join its counterpart in the cooler; and then Jake was on deck once again.

Rubbing my eyes to get the sun and sea mirage from the vision, I was sure I saw a bill slashing in one of the trolling spreads, and then there it was again. Lulled into a trance by a somewhat slow period of trolling, now I was wide awake calling out to the crew. The mate jumped to the stern, pitch bait rod in hand, ready to toss a ballyhoo when the sailfish took to the air after hitting a hooked lure.

The bait was clearly wrapped around its bill, and this time, there would be no submarine battle. Jake was doing battle with a real tail-walker! The fish jumped more times than I can recall. Dancing to the left, running along the starboard side, then racing to the other side, all while we cleared the spread. The mate was at Jake's side, aiding him in his battle. I'm sure the little man wanted to do it himself, but he'd need a couple more years before he could tackle a fish like this on his own.

And what a fish. A bit smaller, in the ninety-to-one-hundred-pound range, still it fought like it was in the heavyweight department. A dragon of a fish, and Jake was the knight who would slay it. Indiana Jones would be proud. Time stood still as the fish neared boatside, and then cheers filled the air. Jake had his first billfish at just ten years old! That night, the celebration would continue at a cool little joint, an old train car set in a hillside and converted into a bar and grill. And of course, the menu consisted of grilled mahi, fried mahi, and blackened mahi, with a touch of Golden mojo. The plane ride home was soon to follow, leaving behind Costa Rica, but taking with us memories to last forever. One day, I hope to add to them.

Chapter 22

The Wayfaring Angler – Mexico, Mayans, and Mermaids

It was 1996, and I needed a passport. Three passports, actually. It had taken me awhile to get here, which wasn't really a surprise. Painting houses at that time wasn't going to put me on the path to the *golden* road; but I had been slinging a brush for many years by then, and really needed a vacation. In those days, Gina, Kasey, and I lived in a mostly poor part of Framingham, Massachusetts. Poor it may have been, but filled with hard workers, including myself. It was a time when going to Florida would stretch the wallet to the breaking point, but here we were planning for Mexico. Kasey was turning seven. Old enough for a real adventure.

I had heard amazing things about the island of Cozumel, just off the Yucatan coast of Mexico. Here the crystal clear, Caribbean waters painted the seascapes, and underwater adventures drew snorkelers and divers to explore its wonders. These same waters abound with fishing opportunities, drawing scores of anglers from all over in search of tuna, Mahi-Mahi, and billfish. So it was that months before, we had put the plan in motion, saving our pennies, and soon May was upon us, and the Yucatan dream would become a reality.

Most of the flight seems but a blur these days, except for landing on the tarmac in Cozumel. I'm not sure if it was a sinus infection or a freak of nature, but as we descended toward the runway, a pain I can only describe as what it must feel like to have an icepick driven through your eyebrow hit me. The pain was practically paralyzing. Slowly, it subsided until I could function again, brushing it off as I could see the worry in Gina and Kasey. Soon, it would be almost forgotten thanks to a welcome margarita as we arrived at our resort. I say almost, but the superstitious freak in me did nurture a bit of worry that it might continue into the rest of the trip. It's easy to imagine why I would've been feeling that way, as I had blown the transmission in my work van just days before we were to depart. But my fear of bad mojo would soon ebb, and cool runnings and calm seas would prevail.

Exploration was tops on the list for the three of us, this being our first trip outside of the United States, and Cozumel didn't disappoint. A nicely appointed, yet cookie-cutter resort, served as home base for our daily excursions, and it suited us just fine for dinner and evening entertainment. There were boat drinks for the adults, kiddie plays for the young ones, and of course, what Mayan resort would be complete without the fire-dancers, the colorfully dressed entertainers expertly juggling torches, brightly-colored and dressed in native-wear of their ancestors from long ago?

The daytime excursions also did not disappoint. There was a day when I rented a jeep and took the family to the furthest stretches of the remote and rugged shoreline along the eastern shore of the island.

Rough, weather-beaten coral ledges, angry but beautiful blue seas under blue skies dotted with cotton balls. And speaking of blue seas, off the west coast of Cozumel lies the second-largest barrier reef, highly regarded amongst the scuba-diving crowd as one the best locations for diving and snorkeling.

A perfect spot to introduce Kasey to the wonders under the sea. But it wasn't just blue. Color swam everywhere. Striped fish, spotted fish, corals in this shade and that, home to sea creatures that grew on their surfaces. Kasey didn't have to find *Nemo*… he was everywhere! And she took to the water like the fish she was swimming with. Effortlessly.

The following day, we got a chance to get out and explore from the topside of the deck on a typical sportfishing boat. At this point, I had yet to do much big-water fishing, and in the mid-nineties, I'm not sure if we even owned a computer yet, so there was no searching the internet for info on the fishing scene. I had billfish on my mind, sailfish in particular, a fish which to that point had only existed in my dreams or TV shows. Nevertheless, we bounced around the Yucatan Channel, rounding out the day with a couple of big Barracuda, and a nice bull mahi for me. It was my first big Dorado, as they're also known in Central and South American waters, and while it was a sizable fish, it's the colors you never forget. Glowing green, yellow, blue, shimmering purple spots. It never gets old. I may have not caught my sailfish, but seeing the happiness in a little seven-year-old's eyes, exploring the tropical seas above and below, more than made up for it. The sailfish would have to wait.

In 2008, over ten years had passed since my last visit to the Yucatan, and within those years came a new beginning. One that began a year and a half prior, in a local bar in my neighborhood of Hopkinton, Massachusetts. Some months earlier, my first marriage dissolved into the history books, and I had relocated nearby to be close to my daughter. Kasey, now far removed from that little girl in Cozumel, was soon to graduate high school, and college bound. Regardless, of course, it was important for me to be nearby.

Needless to say, my recently acquired freedom allowed for me to, as the saying goes, explore new frontiers. The summer of 2006 was party time. It seemed like every other day, my co-workers and I would wrap up work at REZ-1, an intermodal logistics company in Newton, Massachusetts, and make a fast track to Boston.

Sometimes we'd catch happy hour in time for dollar oysters at Faneuil Hall Marketplace, but more often than not we'd end up at the Barking Crab restaurant. The Barking Crab has long been a staple of Boston's seaport area, with its distinct red and yellow tent roof spanning over the outdoor bar and grill area, and overlooking Fort Point Channel. Long before it became dwarfed amongst the shadows of the ever-encroaching seaport expansion and the many hotels, it sat alone on the water's edge, a draw for the after-work crowd.

And girls. Did I mention girls? There may have been a few numbers exchanged during the "sow your oats" period of my impending divorce, but for all the pretty girls I may have seen, it was one in my own backyard that stole my heart, and made me fall in love.

UNTIL THE NEXT TIDE

Her name was Shannon. A stunning, twenty-nine-year-old brunette beauty with big blue eyes and a smile that would brighten up even the darkest depths of Mordor. And the day I first laid eyes on her... she was drunk. Okay, maybe not drunk, but feeling pretty good. And she had a Patriots jersey on! It was like a dream come true. She had gone to New England's home opener in Foxboro with friends and stopped in at our local joint on the way home. The Dynasty restaurant in Hopkinton would seem your standard Chinese restaurant when you first come across it. But on our side of town, with not a whole lot of offerings nearby, it boasted quite a cool bar scene.

In those days, Thursdays, Fridays, and Saturdays, you might have three deep at the bar. Sundays, you got the spillover from the "Sunday Funday" activities. And on that particular day, that's where I was. On the opposite side of the bar, looking at this pretty chick talking to a casual acquaintance, I was captivated. Of course, I made my way over, introduced myself, and struck up a conversation. Immediately, we could feel a spark, a connection, so many things in common, and not just that she too had recently gotten out of a broken marriage, but so many coincidences that weren't coincidences. As it turned out, Shannon had also just picked up a side job, tending bar a couple of nights a week. Those, of course, became the nights I made certain to visit the bar. In a matter of a couple of weeks, we went from just meeting to walking the Marginal Way in Ogunquit, Maine, falling in love at York Harbor Inn, and moving in together.

Well, actually, her cat moved in first. Shannon had taken up temporary residence at her mother's condo after her divorce, and Jay

Kitty came with her. But Mom grew tired of listening to the cat cry all night, as Shannon was spending every night at my place now. With that, I soon became a cat owner (something I swore I would never do... alas, love is blind). Shannon was right behind Jay Kitty, and a few months after our first meeting, our lives would forever change, and be joined during a whirlwind lover's getaway to Key West. She had been feeling extra tired as of late, and even though the weekend had been fueled by partying up and down Duval Street, Shannon suspected there was more at play. In a morning that followed, sitting on a stone wall made of coral, and overlooking the beautiful gulf-blue waters, we discussed the baby now growing inside her. Jack Laurence Golden was born in August of 2007.

Newfound love and a newborn baby can certainly get the rollercoaster of life on the fast track. Sprinkle in a bit of fog and stress, and you may even make some questionable decisions. But, right or wrong, you live with them. For some reason we can't really pin down, maybe it was uncertainty about insurance for the new babe, or worry of the opinions of others (yeah, that may be the most stupid of them), Shannon and I decided to keep our nuptials a secret. And so, what better day to elope than on our country's birthday, July 4th, 2007. One month before Jack's arrival.

We exchanged our private vows of love to one another on a warm summer day in 2007, at the historic Grist Mill in Sudbury, Massachusetts, but the rest of the world would not see us as married until May of 2008. Shannon and I passed our actual honeymoon off as our "babymoon," postponed until after Jack appeared, with

Shannon's mother, Sue, happy to keep watch on the little guy while we celebrated and took some much need time of our own. The plan was to exchange rings at the ancient Mayan ruins of Tulum, and then call home to share that Jack's parents were officially wedded. Playa Del Carmen awaited.

Tropical drinks and howler monkeys greeted us upon our arrival at our resort, the Iberostar Quetzal, and the first day and half was spent soaking up rays, swimming in crystal blue water, smoking Cuban cigars, and drinking cold cervezas. One of our first ventures outside the resort was to Xcaret, an ecological park that has incredible, natural wildlife, Caribbean lagoons, fantastic snorkeling, and ancient Mayan cultural shows. All amazing on their own, but the one thing we were there for was to snorkel through the underground river, in cenote cool water which winds its way through natural passages before emptying in one of the park's Caribbean lagoons.

Mystery, romance, history and tropical fish accompanied us on our swim before we emerged in a blue paradise. We relaxed under the palms with an oversized watermelon margarita made for two, wishing the day would never end. I let my mind go to a place where I was swimming with a mermaid all to myself. But it was not a mere dream. Looking to my left, there she was. Glowing.

The next day I rented a jeep, and we would venture on our own, bound for Tulum, to exchange rings under the eyes of the Mayan Gods. Alright, maybe it wasn't for the Mayan Gods, but it was us, to free ourselves from the secret we had been keeping from family and friends. The idea that we had to keep our marriage a secret now seems

234

foolish, but nevertheless, it's one we live with, and perhaps a renewal of vows will bring us the party we never had. Either way, we were giddy in love, still new even with a diaper genie at home. And on this day, I took Shannon's hand, she took mine, and rings found their new homes on each other's fingers.

The celebration of two continued into the afternoon, as we drove the jeep into the town of Playa Del Carmen, drinking, swinging on bar swings, calling friends and family to share the news, and watching fire dancers on the beach. The night was capped on a beachside chaise lounge bed, with servers bringing tequila and memories. A relaxing day in the sun awaited in the following morn, and of course, no trip to the tropics would be complete without an excursion to the bluewater. The sailfish had waited long enough.

Cinco de Mayo. The fifth of May. Certainly, a day for celebration! Or is it? In the United States, most of us know it as a day to clink a couple of Corona bottles together. A day to party, to celebrate Mexican heritage! As Americans, we'll find any reason to party. Hell yeah, let's celebrate Mexico's independence! But wait. What's that? May 5th isn't Mexico's Independence Day, you say?

No. September 16th is Mexico's actual Independence Day celebration. As it turns out, Cinco de Mayo isn't really a big deal in Mexico outside of Puebla city, where outgunned Mexican forces defeated French troops in a battle that would do little to turn the tide of the conflict with the French.

But for me, balloons floating overhead still made the day feel very festive. Though I'm sure they had simply slipped out of someone's hands, I chose to see the balloons as good luck as they faded into the cloud-speckled blue sky. Shannon and I watched them disappear from the deck of a well-equipped thirtysomething sportfisher, splitting the jetties and leaving the Puerto Aventuras marina in our wake. Incredibly, in what seemed like only a few hundred yards from the beach, the mate was already at work, setting out a spread in our quest for bluewater species, specifically sailfish.

Here, the ocean floor drops away in short time to hundreds of feet, with thousand-foot-plus depths not much further out. Naturally, the bite is seasonal, as in most locations, but had been decent lately, with each day producing a good shot or two at hooking up.

Unlike during my first offshore venture in Yucatan waters some ten years earlier, I now had the internet at my fingertips, and I spent hours researching the area and its opportunities. May happened to a great time to target migrating sailfish in the Yucatan channel.

After scrolling through various reviews, I found an outfit in Puerto Aventuras, a sweet little gated village just south of Playa Del Carmen, and a relatively short drive from our resort. It was managed by a dude from Texas who owned a few sportfishing boats. Typically, I would be hesitant to hire a charter that seemed at first glance not to have the local knowledge that ups your chances for success. Fortunately, one of the great things about charters in Mexico is that while you can own and operate the business, you have to hire locals to work the boat as skipper and deckhands. As it turned out, the captain and mate couldn't have been nicer, and we did our best to work together through broken English and my mangling of Spanish. These guys spoke to the fish in their finest Espanol, and in short time, flying fish were dimpling the deep blue water's surface, skipping like a flat stone tossed on a glass lake.

Freshly caught, Mayan Mahi-Mahi made for a great lunch for my wife and I, dockside in the Yucatan

Shannon and I were taking in the view from the flybridge alongside the captain when the tranquility of the aquarium spreading out before us was broken by chaos taking place behind us. I jumped down immediately, knowing the commotion could only mean one thing. We had a fish in the spread. I spotted the bill slashing at a lure dancing in the curl of the wake left from the churning of the props, and then the sail. A brilliant, purple fan sliced through the waves.

Bright blue pec fins aglow, this fish was hot and lit up. The rigger snapped with a reflecting crack, and we were off to the races.

Unlike my first sailfish in Costa Rica, which played a "stay deep" game, this fish wanted to fly. And fly it did, putting on a spectacular aerial display, waving its flag like a proud soldier pushing back the French army at the Battle of Puebla. I joined the battle, the rod in hand doing its best to handle the violent head shakes as the sailfish fought for its freedom. It took to the sky, followed by a blazing run, and then tail-walked again atop the waves, but the skipper expertly kept us at the right angle, giving us the edge. Some battle-worn minutes later, the mate had the bill in hand. After a quick picture, the valiant warrior was revived and released, to fight another day. Unfortunately, the same would not hold true for the next warrior to enter the spread.

A half-day charter for big game fishing usually wouldn't present the angler with many opportunities to quell the fishing fever, given the restrictions based solely on the limited time at hand. On a trip that started with an early catch of a beautiful seventy-pound Atlantic Sailfish, I figured I had already won the day. But the fish didn't know that. Snap! I heard the line break free of the outrigger at just about the same time as the thirty-plus-pound Mahi-Mahi jumped ten feet in the air, lure flaring from the corner of its mouth. My beautiful bride was next up, but she lovingly gave it up, and I was now tight to a raging bull.

And it was indeed a bullfight. The sailfish fought a tough battle, but this was different. Its power was different—a compact puncher's brawl. While the few jumps I got out of the sail were amazing, what we had here was something completely different. It took about twenty jumps from this angry, fluorescent green and yellow fish for the fight to turn in my favor. I had the good fortune of the hook holding to its purpose. Alas, this big dorado would not earn his freedom, but would be offered up as a feast for us not-so newlyweds. Shannon would cap the half-day trip with another mahi, slightly smaller but not afraid to fly, and an absolute beast of a Barracuda, with teeth that would make Dracula hide in his coffin.

The short trip back to port came with cold Dos Equis cervezas, courtesy of the captain, while the mate skillfully cleaned the mahi for us. We took just enough to enjoy a fresh-caught lunch back at the little, dockside cantina. The rustic tables overlooked the harbor, with a scattering of charter boats along one side. The other side was partially caged off. Here, dolphins played and rolled inside the enclosure, part of an immersive tourist experience, welcoming folks to swim with *Flipper*. From the shade of the thatched hut covering our table, we watched as dolphins jumped in synch and in symphony. We were hypnotized by the grace of these animals that weigh hundreds of pounds moving so fluidly together.

The mahi was soon at our table, prepared simply, grilled and lightly seasoned into bite-sized pieces, and accompanied by a half-dozen amazing sauces—spicy, tangy, hot pepper, sweet, tastes from across the globe to dip in. It was incredible, and we were served the freshest margaritas to wash it all down. To this day, Shannon still gets embarrassed reminiscing about it because she thinks of the light blue bandanna she had wrapped her hair in—she was my Mexican beauty for a day. It was one of the most peaceful moments of my life; and it came on the heels of a great fishing trip, with my love I'd been searching for my whole life, the real catch of a lifetime. I knew someday, we'd return.

After that, I blinked and fourteen years came and went. Memories both good and bad were left in the wake of the ship of time. I lost loved ones, including my mom, who made it just shy of 85 and passed in the shadow of the Covid-19 pandemic. But there were many reasons to celebrate, especially Kasey marrying her love Ethan. We had three more Patriots Super Bowl victories, two Red Sox World Series wins, a Celtics championship, and a Bruins Stanley Cup. Yeah, we had some ups and downs, but Shannon and I had fourteen years to watch Jack grow from the baby boy who stayed home for our last adventure south of the border, through the *Toy Story* years. Those years seemed at times to last forever, but in reality they passed much too quickly. I cherished the era when Jack dressed like Sheriff Woody every day and greeted other patrons at the supermarket with "my name's not Jack, it's Woody!" Or lazy days when we would go to soak power bait at the local pond and I'd give my little buddy a light rod with a small Kastmaster to keep him from getting bored, only to have him yell "Dad, I've got one," as he reeled in a nice rainbow.

And, of course, they were also fourteen years of fish. Big fish, little fish, striped fish, blue fish. But for the fourteen-year-old Jack, no big fish. In those years there were no airplanes, no foreign countries.

That was about to change. It was time to return to the land of the Mayans. The Covid-19 pandemic was edging ever so close to an end. It'll never truly be gone for good, but during the summer of 2021 the world had come to treat and manage covid, and regain some kind of control. Vaccines were working to keep people safe, or at the very least, to minimize the severity of the illness, should you contract the virus. Hospitalizations and deaths were down, and steadily dropping. The world was starting to open back up, and that included travel. People needed to break the cabin fever that had enveloped us for going on two years. Folks yearned to get out. To live again. Shannon and I were no different, and the travel industry was begging people to travel again.

After a bit of back and forth, it was settled. Mexico, we're coming back, and this time we're bringing Jack Golden to your sun-soaked beaches. In February of 2022, Jack boarded his very first flight, and touched down in Cancun, bound for the Mayan Riviera.

The Barcelo resort was more like an enormous compound, but for our first family trip with Jack out of the country, it certainly fit the bill. Shannon's mom, Sue, rounded out the party, and where some would be put off by vacationing with their mother-in-law, Sue not only rounds out the party, she brings the party with her. More than once the words "I love tequila" were heard echoing across the garden pool area, where we lounged during the day. We were on a five-day tropical adventure, and the all-inclusive resort mainly served as home base for our excursions.

Of course, I couldn't take Jack to Mexico without a fishing trip on the list. But first, an adventure under the waters of the Maya awaited. A quick breakfast at the seaside buffet had us set to begin the day, as we boarded a passenger van with a few others who were to embark for the day. Our first stop was a small cenote, sunken in the ground and accessed via a cave. The four of us gathered our snorkeling gear and navigated down the ancient-looking steps into what felt like a sacred place. Amazing stalactites and stalagmites sprouted from the floor and the ceiling, created over thousands of years of water leeching through limestone. We could see caverns under the mirror-clear water, disappearing into the depths, as if we were floating in space with the spirits of ancient civilization surrounding us.

The cenote excursion seemed to end before it began, lost in time, but the snorkeling would continue at our next stop. A tropical lagoon that eventually met the blue of the Caribbean Sea. But that's not to say the clear waters of the lagoon didn't have their own colors. Tropical fish of all shades darted amongst the rocks and deep holes that spotted the sandy curves. Giant parrotfish painted in green and blue were tempting the adventurers under the mirrored surface. It was our own Caribbean aquarium, and we were immersed in it. It was an adventure that had us all smiling, and not even knowing we were doing so.

I have to say, snorkeling and diving under the sea comes a close second for me, a waterman obsessed with fishing. I could do it every day; and while that isn't an option today, I look forward to next time I don a mask and fins. Not surprisingly, my bucket list doesn't just involve checking off another finned species caught, but also swimming with them. Specifically, Whale Sharks, for which, by chance, the Yucatan just happens to be one of the premier destinations.

Isla Mujeres, an island just north of Cancun, hosts an annual migration for these incredible fish, drawing numerous snorkelers to check off an adventure on their own bucket lists. But for me, that adventure is to be pursued another day. On this day, we were taking our smiles to our final stop, a beachside cantina, reserved just for us and our snorkeling companions. The winding, sandy path through the palms and mangroves took us through a checkpoint, basically a gate in the middle of nowhere. The path soon opened to a remote lot, where beachside huts lined the sea.

It was one of the most beautiful spots, and most peaceful settings I've seen, with rolling Caribbean surf, thatched huts, hammocks, and a small beach bar. Picnic tables awaited us, along with incredible margaritas, and tortilla chips with fresh pico de gallo. The only negative was the short time we had at this paradise. If we could've stayed the rest of the trip right on this stretch of beach, I'm not sure anything could've dragged us away. But soon, back at the resort, my thoughts turned to our date with Jeremias, and our charter in the morning with JLC fishing. Avast ye' hearties... There be beasts beneath the waves.

UNTIL THE NEXT TIDE

We awoke to another beautiful day in Mexico, with infinite sunshine. The temperature had been averaging in the low-to-mid-eighties, with mostly low humidity. Nights had been breezy, in the low seventies. Truly perfect weather, the kind we hope for during summers in New England, instead of the recent turn toward ninety-percent humidity. I think we got lucky with the humidity for the tropics, but the only slight concern I had was with the wind. We had a steady breeze, and whitecaps dotted the seas.

Nevertheless, we hopped a taxi to the Puerto Aventuras Marina, where we would meet Jeremias and his twenty-four-foot panga. We made arrangements with our driver, Johnathan, to pick us up after our return, and a nicer guy we had yet to meet. We would ring him from the cantina alongside the dock where the boat was tied up. Jeremias greeted us dockside, along with his mate, and welcomed us aboard. Shannon, Jack, and I rounded out the crew, as Shannon's mom, Sue, opted for poolside relaxation. Probably a good idea, which we would soon understand. As we cleared the jetties, it became clear we were in for a bumpy ride. Lucky for me, my family grows their sea legs quickly. Today would be a test for sure.

It didn't take long for Jack to feel the effects of the six-foot swells. He wouldn't have to reach for the rails at all, never losing his breakfast, but that didn't make the queasiness any better. It made him feel shitty enough to lay midship on the long cooler. Now, in fishing circles around the northeast bars, when you here guys talking four-to-six-foot swells, they're overstating by a couple of feet.

Not here, and not this day. There was a large, perhaps forty-two-foot, sportfisher trolling for billfish in the distance, and the tips of the riggers were skirting the waves with the swells. A short time later, I can't lie, I felt a disturbance in the force. Seasickness is seriously rare for me. My queasiness was short-lived, however, as soon as Jeremias called out "sailfeesh, sailfeesh!" Amigo, we had one in the light spread we were trolling on the way to the reef we would be jigging along.

Alas, the excitement was short-lived. The sail was simply teasing us, and would not surface again, as we crisscrossed the waves. Our journey continued to the first stop along the reef, where I grabbed the heavy spinning rod, and began working a jig furiously to entice and Amberjack or grouper that may be in residence. I had my heart set on catching a big AJ, as Jeremias is well-known locally as an AJ expert; but unfortunately, we were in a transitional season, and they were hard to come by at this time. Jig, drop, jig, drop, on and on. Speed jigging is a deadly technique, where you jig quite fast just off the bottom, interspersed with cranking a handful of feet, then releasing and repeating.

After repeated attempts, however, it became clear the "right" species wasn't home. There was a decent triggerfish spot nearby, and the captain put us on it in no time. I continued to work the heavy jig, while Jack, feeling slightly better, took to the rail to drop some bait. In short time, he was rewarded with his first of two triggerfish on the day. Nothing giant, but it had taken the skunk off the boat. Now, it was time to wipe it clean. The three of us grabbed rods, and soon we were jigging up smaller fish like snappers. It was the ammo we needed to break out the heavy gear.

Jeremias got Jack situated, threw a snapper on a heavy Penn rod, and sank the nervous bait to the depths. In what seemed like seconds, the heavy rod was arching under the weight of a big fish, the line peeling from the big gold reel. Jack was mustering his teenage strength, and gaining, albeit inch by inch, when Shannon took over to take her shot. The big Reef Shark wasn't taking it easy on her; and Jeremias upped her chances by kicking the reel down into low-gear, which eases the cranking for the angler, but prolongs the battle, as you now take up much less line with each crank. Swapping back and forth, Jack battled the fish to the surface, and after a few pics, we revived and released a beautiful, one-hundred-twenty-pound shark. I took advantage of the break in the action, continuing to jig, and was rewarded with a fresh Yellowtail Snapper that I quickly reworked on the jig as bait. I was on only seconds after I dropped it down from the big reel.

Once again, the rod bucked, doubled over with the weight of a beast. I tried to hasten the battle, kicking the reel into high gear, and while I was gaining line, it quickly evaporated in the kick of a large tail. Jack and I went to work, with me subbing for Shannon on this round. Father and son, and sore shoulders, eventually bested the hundred-fifty-pound shark, which was rewarded with his freedom for a battle well fought. Big fish and big waves. No AJ for me, and I didn't care. Doing what I love, and sharing it with my family, rough seas and all, made it all worth it.

Back at the dock, we said our praises to Jeremias, gifted him with the couple of triggerfish we caught, and settled in at the cantina for a couple of cold cervezas and a Coca Cola, and waited on our taxi. The rest of our stay was spent under the palms, recalling our adventures and thinking about the next one. I pondered the miles of water covered, the miles of sand walked, and the memories in the wake. The one I like the best is the next one I get to share with my kids. Jack may never become a certified "fishing fool" like his Dad, but I know he loves to go with me, and gets just as excited when he hooks up. I mean, let's face it, the hours between bites can be grueling on the psyche; but man, it wakes up fast when a good fish finds your bait. With that in mind, I've got something in the works for Jack and me next season, where I hope to put him on some giant stripers.

Chapter 23

Back to the Future

Many moons ago, and many decades even further back from that, George McFly uttered those famous words "I am your density," when trying to woo his future beloved Lorraine, until Biff rudely interrupted his attempt at "destiny." Little did he know what the future would hold, or what this future would play in his past. For this salty dog, the future represents the ever-moving evolution of the tides, but also a chance to share my adventures with those who one day may cast into the same waters. A chance to leave an imprint, a memory, or a desire to reel in finned behemoths of the deep.

But those memories usually don't start with sea monsters. Usually, they start with tidal ponds and silversides. Lily pads and sunfish, or maybe clam bits and sea robins. Looking inward at my future these days, more often than not, I find that it reflects the past, where wide-eyed kids marveled at the wriggling fish on the end of the line. You see, part of any angler's evolution sooner or later includes the role as "teacher" to the next generation. A way to keep the love of the sea alive, to pass on the need to be a responsible steward, but to also show the pure enjoyment a simple fishing rod and reel can bring to ones' life.

For me, it started on a pier in Lynn catching flounder, or catching hornpout at the neighborhood reservoir. For my part, the smiles I helped put on the faces of the young ones in my life are part of the reward of my own evolution.

Kasey was about eleven years old when I convinced her mother to let her skip school, a chance to play hooky and go fishing with her dad. The Striped Bass were in the middle of their Fall migration, and the weather on this late September day called for sunblock and seaworms. It was seventy-five degrees, and there wouldn't be many more chances this year for a kid to don a bathing suit and splash around on a warm, Indian summer day. Kasey and I got to the narrow inlet in Cotuit, Massachusetts, where a small beach hugged the channel, and I set up an eight-foot surfrod with a small hook and seaworm, with an egg sinker to hold bottom.

Digging in the sand at the ocean's edge, drip castles began to take form when she immediately took notice of the rod tip bouncing under the pull of a nice bass, while I was pre-occupied with setting up another rod. I dropped what I was doing and raced to her side, grabbing the rod, waiting on the tug of the line, and setting the hook, all the while showing her what I was doing. Handing the rod off, she laughed, but then the smile turned serious. Kasey wanted this fish. Her smile returned, with a sense of achievement, as she slid the big schoolie bass onto shore. Now with her grin running ear to ear, we posed for a couple of fish selfies, before letting the bass swim off to freedom. It wasn't long before she was back at it, this time taking the lessons from the first fish and putting them to good use. The morning

249

continued with non-stop action as waves of migrating stripers moved through. Somewhere in there is room for a dad joke about putting the "hook" in playing hooky. Bad? Yeah, I know. But great all the same.

By the time next summer rolled around, Kasey was now a full-fledged tweener, which can be good and bad, depending on whether you're talking about teenage attitude, or that sweet-spot where kids still like to hang with their parents. But physically, they also take a jump in their composure, coordination, and smarts. On a day early in the summer, she put it all together on a family trip to the South Cape Beach in Mashpee.

Somehow, I convinced her and her mother to make the long walk to the Waquoit jetty, where bass and blues had been quite active. Of course, I toted most of the supplies, cooler, fishing gear, the works. But summer was here, and as New Englanders, we needed to take advantage of every minute. Arriving at the jetty, we set out our beach blanket and settled in for a relaxing day in the sun. Kasey was more than happy to accompany me on the jetty, making the mostly-easy walk over the big flat stones to the section that had many years earlier been broken by a storm.

With the tide running west, the jetty is a great spot to cast for Bluefish, especially early in the season. On this day, the blues were nowhere to be seen, but Kasey was about to put her newfound, twelve-year-old maturity on display. I had set her up with a surfrod, and a five-inch swimming plug—a Yo-Zuri crystal minnow in chartreuse. Just to the left of where we were standing atop the rocks, what appeared to be a chunk of the jetty was some yards offshore, now covered in wavering seagrass, taunting us to cast. Kasey fired a cast with the aim that belied her experience and age. Whether from experience or luck, or a combination of both, she put the lure right on the edge of the dark clump, and began a steady retrieve. A few cranks in, and she was tight to a decent striper. The next cast proved that this was not merely luck, but evolution. Another bass was fooled by the darting lure. Kasey would pull a couple more bass off the structure until it seemed we had exhausted the locals. Meanwhile, I don't recall ever firing a cast myself while I enjoyed the show and tried to hide my pride.

Occasionally, the smiles weren't as easy to come by. Being the fishin' fool that I am, I've always wanted to share my love for the sea and the creatures that live in it, and try to pass it on. On a family vacation many summers ago, my brother Chris and I planned a Striped Bass charter out of Kennebunkport, to introduce his sons Nicholas and Daniel to sportfishing. Also with us was Jake, my sister Erin's son. Now Jake, growing up in Truro on Cape Cod, had a bit o' salt in his blood, and took to the sea with ease. For Nicholas and Daniel, it was a new world. One that started with smiles as we jigged up tinker mackerel and baby pollack, soon to be used as bait for big bass. Puffing my chest as the cool Uncle, I was feeling pretty good about getting my nephews out fishing. But, shortly after we left the bait jigging behind, we moved into the shallows, which shall we say, was a bit more sporty, and got the twenty-one foot center console rocking.

Nicholas and Daniel, being respectively eight and six years old, quietly came down with a case of the knee-knocking nerves. By the time we were bouncing along the surfline, the little guys were literally sitting on the deck, as if the watchman on the Titanic had just yelled "iceberg...dead ahead!" While I was happy reeling in stripers in the mid-thirty-inch range, a part of my heart was aching. Had I put them in the wash too early? One of these days, we'll revisit the Maine surf and give it another go, but years after that first boat trip, Plum Island welcomed us from a surfcaster's view.

When the boys were still young, we'd head to the North shore to visit my brother and family, and spend a few hours at the beach. Of course, being the salty dog I was, we couldn't simply go out to the beachfront, and slap on the Coppertone. No, we needed to stop at Surfland Bait and Tackle and check in with the proprietor Kay. Here, we'd pick up some fresh clams and a mackerel or two, and head to the mouth of the Merrimack River. When the kids were still little, the day was basically a designated beach outing where I'd toss out some clams, and spike the rod. An occasional schoolie would bend a rod here and there, giving the kids brief moments of excitement. The years would pass, and then one year, the nerves of that trip to Kennebunkport long past, Daniel was now approaching twenty years when a family trip to Plum Island lined up with a dropping tide at the river mouth.

It was early June, prime time for Striped Bass, and the famous, if not infamous, sandbar close to the entrance of the river was historically one of the best spots to fish. Daniel was anxious to give it a go, which was exciting for me to see, as Dan was more scientist than adventurer; but gone was the little kid nervously bouncing in the

Maine surf. Now, here he was, surfrod in hand, following his uncle closely, through some turbulent current, barefoot, bathing suits, and a bag of clams. Dan and I made our way to the middle of the river where our casts would just reach the tip of the sandbar. The first cast tumbled in the current, dropping into the deeper water, and in short time, Dan was tight to a striper.

A couple more fish would find the clams to their liking before it was my time for the nerves to kick in. The current in this location can be dangerous to say the least, and as the tide continued to bottom out, I didn't want to take any chances with my nephew. Honestly, even though we didn't catch any giants, it truly was one of the most satisfying outings, one I hope Dan thinks of when his uncle can no longer cross that sandbar.

Fast forward a decade and a half, and getting back to the future, my son Jack, now sixteen years old (as of these words being put to paper), is like most kids these days, where it's easy to get lost in a world of gaming and social media. But Jack has something a lot of the other kids don't have. If he plays the role of Marty McFly, then I'm his Doc Brown, looking forward to taking him on new adventures. Our expeditions take us to a world of blue skies, clean air, and calm seas. Sure, the flux capacitor, aka his cell phone, still fills in the downtime when the action is dragging; but he's got a bit of the sea in his blood. I think he might've been all of two weeks old when I first dipped his feet in the ocean off Ogunquit Beach.

As for the actual fishing part, while the adventure for him is not so much about catching, but about being with his dad, I'm not sure he realizes the best part of these adventures for me is knowing we are making memories together. While all this is true, I do look forward to the day when he lands his first trophy fish. Lucky for him, he's a natural at the basics. The casting part came easy for him. I don't think it took more than a few demonstrations, and he was casting long and on target. The catching would come.

I recall a particular day trip to catch trout at Peter's Pond in Sandwich, on Cape Cod. Uncle John (Rice), as Jack has grown up calling him, and I had taken him many times through the years to catch trout. Usually this meant reeling in the power-bait caught trout we had already hooked. It was really more cranking the fish in than anything else. The hooking part was already done.

Well, this day, John and I were readying to set up a couple of bait rods, and I wanted to keep young Jack from getting bored, so I gave him a rod with a small, gold Kastmaster, thinking he'll enjoy just casting. "Dad…I've got one!" soon echoed through the trees. Jack had hooked up a nice rainbow in just a couple of casts! His first fish on an artificial lure! I was so excited for him, maybe even more so than he was. My day was already set, but far from over. Every few minutes, as we were waiting on hits on the bait rods, Jack would get a hit, and landed a couple more.

To outside observers, that day would've made it seem easy; but Jack knows all too well that there are those days when boredom takes over. Sure, when he was a little boy, a tub of earthworms and hungry panfish would keep even the most hard-to-please kids from getting sleepy-eyed, but eventually, you want to up the game. Where are the big fish?

This is when it gets harder, even with bait. Big shiners to tempt big bass and big trout. Wachusett reservoir fish. Or beasts from the salty seas. While Jack has had his share of cranking in big fish like a forty-one-pound Smallmouth Bass he caught in recent years, he has yet to go A-to-Z, meaning baiting, casting, setting the hook, and landing, completely on his own. I mean, sure, he can put a worm on a hook and cast out his float to the edge of some lily pads, but I'll admit I've been somewhat lax in teaching him the technical basics. The most important knots, the terminal tackle, how to truly read the water and the surrounding shoreline.

As a Dad, I was focused on just putting him on the action. He's watched and observed as I baited, battled, and landed seventy-pound Spinner Sharks in Captiva, Florida from the beach. He's assisted with the giant Bluefish and bass from the sands of Cape Cod. I have to admit, some of my favorite memories are of me helping him hold the rod while he cranked the reel with two hands. Over the rail, on a boat out of Bud n' Mary's marina in the Florida Keys, this little kid was happily swinging schoolie-sized Mahi-Mahi onto the deck. Of course, with Cape Cod in our backyard, some decent stripers would follow, as would nice sea bass and Fluke. More recently, as a fourteen-year-old, he battled hundred-plus-pound Reef Sharks in Florida. But now I look to pass on the salty knowledge that so many of today's youth are missing out on.

This year, I'm already dreaming up the expeditions we'll embark on, including a proper introduction to giant Striped Bass found offshore. In the spring, I'm looking to get him on his own bass inshore, wading up inside the salt ponds, tossing topwater plugs, dancing spooks, and jumpin' minnows. Tying knots, reading the water, and understanding the tides. Memories to keep of his dad wanting to share his passion, and one day, using those memories to teach his own kids the ways of the water.

Chapter 24

What Next?

We all dream. Some you remember. Some you don't. All fishermen and fisherwomen undoubtedly dream in varying shades of blue. It's unavoidable if you find yourself in a life-long love affair with the sea. But the waking dreams that run wild during the day? That's the fun part, right? Like when the lottery reaches an astronomical number. You fantasize about what you'd do with your millions. A luxury car. A tricked-out mega-sportfisher. Worldly destinations, otherwise only a dream. The Seychelles. The Maldives. Bora Bora. Perhaps a mother-ship fishing trip to the Great Barrier Reef of Australia.

These bucket list fantasies may or may not be attainable in my life, as the story is still being written, but this fishing fool can still look at what's next. I've been fortunate to have quite a few sea monsters pay me a visit over the years, and the adventures they took me on in my quest to find them. But in those pages that may come to print in future chapters of my life, there are new adventures I look toward, to fill them.

I'm looking forward to sharing more adventures with my son, particularly in the salt, but whether it's for those trips that see Jack accompanying me, or if I'm solo, I'm determined to add a new tool to the tackle tool belt. A flyrod! I'm a man on a mission, possibly difficult, but not impossible. Now, I'm not completely new at the fly game, but I may as well be. I've dabbled with flyfishing at the novice level, and I can cast okay, but compared to those pros I see online and on TV—where double-hauling basically puts their fly in the surfcaster's territory—I'm a total newbie.

I've managed to catch a few schoolie Striped Bass. These fish were laying in a rip line coming off the corner of a deck sticking out in the Bass River on Cape Cod. Hardly what I would call challenging. But this spring, I'm toting my flyrod up inside a southside bay on the Cape, where there is a bottleneck. In recent years, we discovered this destination as a great, early season spot where the herring get pinched flooding into the upper bay, and the schoolies are right on their heels.

Topwater plugs have proven irresistible on these hungry fish, and I'm betting a fly darting through the upper channel will also draw strikes. Later in May, I'm targeting the outer beaches of the Cape, when the bass make their way north around Memorial Day, chasing sandeels along the edge of the troughs that run the beach. And then, in the Fall, when albie fever takes over, and after my first fish of the season is landed on spinning gear (the fever won't let me switch to the flyrod before I catch at least one little tunny), I'll be looking for my first silver bullet.

Whatever the outcome, I'm planning on taking a fly outfit on almost every surfcasting trip this year, if the weather allows it. Some of the trips that I'm planning are more specialized, and not suited for the flyrod, being shore-based shark trips. Sharks have always been swimming and feeding just off Cape Cod's beaches, and they've become quite popular during the warmer summer months, with Brown Sharks the primary target. Brown Sharks can reach two hundred pounds. Though most would be considerably smaller, a hundred-pound shark would not be a surprise. I'm not a newbie when it comes to shore-based shark fishing, having caught several in Florida, but I've yet to give it a real go in the northeast. This will make quite an adventure on a starlit night for Jack and me—as this is predominantly a night bite—and I have a perfect spot lined up, where I've seen sharks cruising during early summer afternoons.

Speaking of Jack, in the last chapter, I mentioned getting him on his first, giant Striped Bass, and my plan is to get us out to Block Island, dropping black eels into the depths. This would not only be an adventure for him, but for me as well, as my one and only trip to "the Block" was less than bountiful. That first week of November, over two decades ago, saw John Rice and I book a charter for a day that some Captains would call "sporty." Let's just say, the spin cycle on a washing machine is less sporty than that day was, a day in which we watched the mate lose his lunch over the side while John and I held fast to whatever was nailed down in the cockpit. One blue and one bass hardly made up for the angry seas. Nevertheless, years later, it has me looking to return to these fabled waters, but this time in what should be the warm and calm waters of a summer evening. If the fish gods are with us, a new fish tale will be entered into the memory bank of a father and son.

As for what lies beyond the coming year, my bucket list still has an extensive array of species waiting to be checked off. An adventure

UNTIL THE NEXT TIDE

I've been itching to go on is a trip to upstate New York and the salmon and trout runs of late autumn. Social media pics of giant Brown Trout and salmon, and, not long after, steelhead, stir an envy I'm usually not subjected to, leaving me wanting to explore these historical tributaries of Lake Ontario. In the coming years, I plan on wading these rivers and hope to wrap my hand around the giant tails I see in the online posts from fellow anglers. And then, of course, the Florida Keys are always beckoning me to return. While I will always treasure the dances I've had with the silver king, Tarpon are not the only game in town, and high on my list are two gamefish that make up the other two fish on the "Grand Slam"—the giant silver dollar, aka the Permit, and the grey ghost of the flats, the Bonefish.

A return to the Pacific coast of Costa Rica, where I hope to finally wrest a giant Roosterfish from the surf, also holds a place on the list. Then there are marlin off the coast of Hawaii, where John currently resides, and giant Yellowfin Tuna on the offshore oil rigs of the Gulf of Mexico.

The list is long, and as Captain Quint would say, "daylight's wastin'!" For now, until the next tide, I'll see you in the suds!

A giant Connecticut River Striped Bass, courtesy of Captain Joe Diorio (above), slow-trolling live bunker with my son, Jack (below).

Jamie Golden is a long-time IT Professional, and contributing writer for some of New England's most prominent sportfishing publications, including *The Fisherman* and *On The Water* magazines.

His adventures have taken him from his home waters of Cape Cod, north to the ragged coast of Maine, and south to the jungles of Costa Rica. Golden currently lives in Hopkinton, Massachusetts with his wife Shannon, and their teenage son, Jack, with his stepdaughter Kasey, son-in-law Ethan, and newly-arrived grandson Sam, residing nearby.

www.ingramcontent.com/pod-product-compliance
Lightning Source LLC
Chambersburg PA
CBHW052034090426
42739CB00010B/1902